TAKE YOUR COMPANY PUBLIC!

TAKE YOUR COMPANY PUBLIC!
The Entrepreneur's Guide to Alternative Capital Sources

Drew Field

New York Institute of Finance

New York London Toronto Sydney Tokyo Singapore

Library of Congress Cataloging-in-Publication Data
Field, Drew.
    Take your company public! : the entrepreneur's guide to
alternative capital sources / Drew Field.
        p. cm.
    Includes bibliographical references and index.
    ISBN 0-13-882242-5
    1. Going public (Securities). 2. Stocks—Marketing.
3. Corporations—Finance.   I. Title.
HG4028.S7F54   1991
658.15′224—dc20   90-32447
                                                                CIP

This publication is designed to provide accurate and authoritative information in regard to the subject matter covered. It is sold with the understanding that the publisher is not engaged in rendering legal, accounting, or other professional service. If legal advice or other expert assistance is required, the services of a competent professional person should be sought.

From a Declaration of Principles
Jointly Adopted by
a Committee of the American Bar Association
and a Committee of Publishers and Associations

© 1991 by NYIF Corp.
Simon & Schuster
A Paramount Communications Company

Printed in the United States of America
10 9 8 7 6 5 4 3 2 1

To Gwendolyn

Contents

Preface

Money for your company's growth is available from the largest pool of capital in the world. It can be had at zero interest and need never be repaid. It comes free of restrictions on how you run your business.

American households are ready, willing, and able to invest billions of dollars in the shareownership of businesses. They have not been doing that. This book explains why. Then it shows how to get that money, on those terms, through direct marketing of corporate shares.

The reason we are not buying corporate shares is that we are not being sold corporate shares.

We are not being sold corporate shares because that role has been left exclusively to the securities industry, which no longer appears to have either the interest or the ability to market shares to American households.

Chapter 1 of this book tells how Wall Street has changed, how it is no longer a readily accessible channel through which money can flow from individuals to businesses through shareownership.

Chapter 2 shows that the money is really there and—just as important—that we "consumers" are ready to be sold on putting our money into shareownership.

Not every business is a candidate for a public share offering. Chapter 3 helps you decide whether it is right for your business. Chapter 4 explains how the securities industry does an underwritten public offering, and when that may still be the way to go.

The how-to of a direct public offering is discussed in Chapter 5, the most important chapter of this book. You are led through each step, from the day you decide to go forward to the day when all of the money is in and you have hundreds, or thousands, of fellow shareowners.

There is a special section on The Small Corporate Offering Registration (SCOR)—the simplified process for raising up to $1 million a year through direct public share offerings.

The Bibliography suggests books on public offerings, corporate finance, and direct marketing. It includes a commentary on how to use the resources in the Bibliography effectively.

In the extensive Glossary, you can find out what you need to know about corporate shares, public offerings, and direct share marketing.

The message is this: The money is there for your business, on the best possible terms. But the old ways of getting it are not working any more. A new way—direct marketing—will work. Here is how.

You can use this book in several different ways. If you are fairly new to the subject of public shareownership, then a front-to-back reading is recommended. Should you know enough to doubt the premises—that individuals will invest but the mechanism is not currently accessible to them— then Chapter 1 and 2 may help you to believe these premises are true.

You may own a business now and wonder if going public is the right objective. Perhaps you dream of becoming an entrepreneur, but are blocked by the thought of being choked by a shortage of equity capital. Or you may be a lawyer or other advisor to these entrepreneurs or would-be entrepreneurs. Chapter 3 provides the tools for deciding whether public shareownership is the right path for you.

If an underwritten public offering is in the cards for your business, or if you have always wondered what the mystery of going public was all about, Chapter 4 should cast light on the process. For those of you who are ready to get down to it, Chapter 5 can guide you through a direct public offering.

You can dip into the subject at any point, by turning to the Glossary. Virtually everyone, from complete novices in the world of business to corporate securities or direct marketing professionals, will find the Glossary useful. It joins the inside terms of these two specialties and defines them in the context of direct share marketing.

The following sections summarize the book's chapters a little more fully.

WHY SO FEW CORPORATIONS DO UNDERWRITTEN IPOs

Shares of more than ten thousand corporations are being bought and sold in the public trading markets. Nearly every one got there through an underwritten initial public offering (IPO). Entrepreneurs once came to the securities industry because it had the customers, the stockbrokers, and the experience in selling shares to individual investors.

Today, only a token few entrepreneurs make it through the underwritten IPO process. Those who do go public may find that they then share ownership in their corporations with a few institutions and speculators. Why? The supply of money from individuals is there, and entrepreneurs have a strong demand for equity capital. What keeps supply and demand from matching? The reason so few corporations do underwritten IPOs is that the old mechanism—the underwriting syndicate—is not functioning the way it used to. It seems that investment bankers currently find more profit in rearranging and dismantling, and that brokers who specialize in selling stock to individuals are a vanishing breed. Institutional money managers appear to have displaced individual investors as the Street's most significant customers. Complex new financial instruments, such as options and asset securitizations, now compete powerfully with common stock as the basic product of the securities industry.

More undermining to underwritten IPOs than changes in customers and products has been the shrinking of the securities industry. Firms have been disappearing steadily, through liquidations and mergers, since the early 1970s. Among those hardest hit have been the firms that once sold IPOs to individual investors.

Like war and its generals, marketing shareownership is too important to be left to the securities industry—especially if it has largely deserted the field. Chapter 1 of the book presents the case that (1) the decline in the number of individuals buying shares has been caused by changes in the securities industry and (2) Wall Street has not lately shown either the interest or the capacity to raise equity capital through selling shares to individuals.

THE TIME IS RIGHT TO MARKET CORPORATE SHARES

Now is actually a very good time to be going public. Aside from the preoccupation of institutional money managers with short-term results, investment decisions are not made based on the current stage of the business cycle. A basic truth is that, when held for several years, corporate shares have consistently been the best investment. Direct marketing is all about finding the individuals who will see the long-term potential of a company and reaching them with an effective marketing program.

Owning shares in an entrepreneurial corporation fits with some of the major trends that will likely be with us for the next several years. Chapter 2 looks at the changes taking place in six major areas—people's personal values, politics, economics, finance, technology, and work ethic. Together, these changes will encourage individual shareownership of entrepreneurial corporations.

Chapter 2 examines each of these six trends. Much of this chapter is opinion. You may disagree. It is presented as food for thought and as a rationale for making the decision that you can successfully market your company's shares directly to the American public.

In Chapter 2 you can find the themes for your own direct share marketing programs. Wall Street has perennially given us credit for only two motivations: fear and greed. But now marketing of consumer goods and services has gone well beyond fear and greed into the hierarchy of human needs and unconscious desires.

Honest, fair and effective direct share marketing programs have only to draw on this ready knowledge and developed art.

IS PUBLIC OWNERSHIP RIGHT FOR YOUR CORPORATION?

The balance of the book is directed to the entrepreneur who has a business, or an idea for a business. Chapter 3 is presented to help an entrepreneur decide if public ownership fits both the corporation and the objectives and personality of the entrepreneur. We begin with 20 questions, intended to help the entrepreneur (as well as corporate directors, lawyers and advisors) face some facts about the business and some issues of personal motivation.

Pathways are provided that help to answer the questions: "How much money can I raise?" and "What percentage of my company do I have to sell?" Sometimes the answer is that more time and development is needed before going public makes sense.

Beyond the numbers analysis come the twin issues: "Is my company an attractive investment proposition?" and "Am I suited to sharing ownership of my business with the public?" Chapter 3 will help you find the answers.

HOW AN UNDERWRITTEN IPO IS DONE

There are some instances when an underwritten IPO may be available and may work. Chapter 4 explains how an underwritten IPO is done, where this method began, and household assets and deposits do not, however, necessarily translate into money that could be invested in corporate shares. There is risk to consider: Savings accounts will always give back what we deposit—stocks may return more or less. What do we know about the supply of money for risk investment in new issues of corporate shares?

Individuals Have the Money to Buy Corporate Shares. One indication of what is available for share-ownership is the level of so-called discretionary income, the amount left over after paying for a "comfortable living," as defined by the U.S. Census Bureau. Since the early 1960s, the number of American households with significant discretionary income has doubled. By 1987, these people had $320 billion of annual income they did not need just to live well. How much of that money is really available for taking risks? One indicator is the $210 billion that Americans put into legalized gambling in 1988. Another $40 billion or so is estimated to have been bet illegally, mostly on sports. True, gambling money gets recycled quickly, while cash put into stock investments is used in the business. But gambling activity is increasing at the rate of 10% per year.

Individuals Have Largely Cashed Out of Corporate Shares

Since the late 1950s, individuals have consistently received more cash out of the stock market than they have put into it. In the four years through 1988, household investment in corporate shares declined at the rate of $100 billion each year. Much of this money was returned to investors because of cash takeovers or management buyouts. More came from management use of corporate funds to repurchase shares, as a way to increase earnings per share by decreasing the number of shares. When investors received all this cash, they did not recommit it to shareownership. In 1988, when nearly $100 billion came out of stocks, there was a $200 billion increase in savings accounts. Amounts invested in debt securities grew by $450 billion.

Entrepreneurial Corporations Are Ready to Go Public

The low level of IPOs is not because of a lack of entrepreneurs. The rate of new corporations being formed has gone from some 100,000 a year in 1950 to more than 700,000 in 1986—this rate has better than doubled since 1975. Most incorporated businesses will never be candidates for public shareownership. But seven times as many new corporations are being formed, while the number of IPOs has gone down. Entrepreneurs have become a major market for services—magazines have been built around them. Major accounting firms have created separate units to serve them. Banks have developed "middle market" strategies for lending to entrepreneurs.

Why Supply and Demand Are Not Being Matched

Individuals have a plentiful supply of money available to risk in growing corporations. More and more entrepreneurs have been starting their own businesses, creating an increasing need for shareowner capital. If only one in a hundred of the companies incorporated in the 1980s were to go public in its tenth year, the annual rate of IPOs would be more than 6,000. If individuals could be persuaded to part with just ten cents of every dollar of discretionary income, there would be $30 billion for investment in shareownership. That could provide each of those 6,000 businesses with $5 million in new capital.

So why is that not happening? If you believe the supply is there, in the accumulated assets and discretionary income of individual Americans; if you believe that entrepreneurs are being held back by a lack of shareowner capital; then what is keeping the entrepreneurs and individual investors from getting together? The reason supply and demand are not meeting is because the old market mechanism is no longer directed at individuals. Underwriting syndicates do not appear to have the capacity to match supply and demand: A new market is needed.

Let us take a look at how an underwritten IPO is done, and then see why this method is not working as well as it did.

WHAT HAPPENED TO UNDERWRITTEN IPOs

The structure of an underwritten IPO has not changed much since the 1920s. An entrepreneur signs a letter of intent with investment bankers, who are in the corporate finance department of a securities broker-dealer firm. That firm becomes the managing underwriter and organizes an underwriting syndicate with other securities firms. They all employ stockbrokers, who sell the shares by telephoning their customers and prospects.

An underwriting syndicate is a pyramid sales structure, organized around a single transaction. You can see it reflected in the tombstone newspaper announcements of completed underwritings. At the top is the managing underwriter, with any co-managers placed off to the right. Next down the pyramid are members of the underwriting syndicate, arranged in tiers, from major to submajor Wall Street firms, followed by regional brokerages and then local ones.

The power of an underwritten IPO has been this pyramid, the underwriting syndicate. With a syndicate of 50 firms, the strength of 20,000 brokers can be made available. If one in ten of these brokers completed just one $10,000 sale, an underwriting of $20 million could be sold to 2,000 individual shareowners.

Erosion has damaged the underwriting syndicate at all of its levels. It no longer commands the attention it once did of investment bankers at the top of the pyramid; the middle has been depleted as securities firms have disappeared and, at the pyramid's base, brokers are busy selling products other than stocks. In April 1978, William R. Hambrecht,

general partner in Hambrecht & Quist, a leading IPO underwriting firm, testified in Los Angeles before the SEC for its
Examination of the Effects of Rules and Regulations on the
Ability of Small Business to Raise Capital. Among his remarks were these:

> The public was burned by promotional issues in the
> 1960s. . .;
>
> institutions dominate today's market. . . ;
>
> the small broker has almost disappeared, and the large
> investment banking firms are not interested in small
> issues. . . .

To these reasons we can add three more: (1) Products pro-
moted by the securities industry have changed from stocks
to futures, options, and other new financial instruments.
(2) Wall Street makes money today from businesses that are
very different from yesteryear's intermediaries between entrepreneurs and individual investors. (3) Most important,
individuals are no longer customers of the securities industry in the way they once were. What all of these changes get
down to is that *we are not buying corporate shares because they are not being sold to us.* The reasons why so few
corporations now go public begin with the general shrinking and concentration of the securities industry.

THE STREET GETS NARROWER

During the boom times for IPOs, hundreds of securities
broker-dealer firms had corporate finance departments,
staffed with investment bankers. They went searching for
product by calling on private companies in the industries
that were popular with investors. Then, Keith Funston was
president of the New York Stock Exchange (NYSE), leading

a large and successful advertising and promotion campaign for individuals to "Own Your Share of America."

Since the 1960s, underwritten IPOs have become an ever-tighter bottleneck for the flow of capital from individuals to entrepreneurs. The securities firms that once filled out underwriting syndicates have largely disappeared. Those remaining have increasingly moved into different businesses. At all levels of the pyramid, from investment bankers through underwriting syndicates, down to stockbrokers and their individual customers, the infrastructure for underwritten IPOs has been critically weakened. And there is no telling whether the securities industry will ever recommit to making a priority of marketing corporate shareownership between entrepreneurs and individual investors.

Always a cyclical business, the securities industry has suffered waves of mergers and liquidations every three years or so since the early 1960s. In 1961, member firms of the NYSE reached a peak number, 681. They were "the Club," the firms with the size and stature to participate in underwriting syndicates. The rules of the NYSE fixed the rates for trading stocks, prohibiting any price competition. As ways were found to get around fixed trading rates, exchange membership began to decline, to 505 by 1975, when fixed commissions on the NYSE were deregulated into the free market. Three years later, there were 465 member firms.

Smaller brokerages, which were not NYSE members, could once have been counted on to fill the "selling groups" that sold shares to local customers. In 1961, there were 4,700 nonmember firms, but by 1977, only 2,800 remained in business. The effect of this narrowing of Wall Street was described by three chairmen of the Securities Industry Association. In the words of David Hunter, chairman, in an October 9, 1977 *New York Times* article: "Looking at it from the standpoint of the nation as a whole, I'm concerned that the industry is shrinking to a point where it may not perform one of its major functions—capital raising for business." Hunter's successor, Robert Baldwin, head of Morgan Stanley & Co., remarked for a November 6, 1977 *Los Angeles Times* study that: "We are letting America's capital-raising mechanism deteriorate. Sometimes the destruction seems deliberate." Finally, I. W. Burnham II, a founder of Drexel Burnham Lambert, and Mr. Hunter's predecessor as SIA chairman, said in an August 21, 1977 *San Francisco Examiner* report: "We're shrinking. Our ability to finance corporate America is being weakened."

Waves of consolidation have continued. Their end was prematurely described by Chris Welles in his 1975 book, *The Last Days of the Club* (New York: Dutton), and 1981 gave rise to a book titled *The Year They Sold Wall Street,* by Tim Carrington (Boston: Houghton Mifflin, 1985). Since the October 1987 stock market crash, another cycle of mergers and liquidations has been underway. 1989 was the third year in a row of no growth in revenues for the securities industry.

TRANSFORMATION AT THE TOP OF THE SYNDICATE

Investment bankers bring in the corporate clients and manage the stock offering for the underwriting syndicate. Investment bankers have needed the brokers and traders to sell shares, while the brokers and traders have needed the investment bankers to manufacture new product. This relationship of the investment banker "brains" and the retail broker "brawn" has largely come undone. Moreover, "bought deals" have to some extent replaced the syndicate, and "soft dollar" orders have done the same to syndicate sales.

Syndicate Brains versus Brawn

Status and power among Wall Street investment bankers is signified by the tombstone ads that announce a completed underwriting. Copies of the ads are embedded in acrylic for display on desks and conference tables. They are made into wall plaques. Tombstone reprints on slick paper appear in packets given to prospective investment banking clients.

At the top of the underwriting syndicate pyramid in these tombstones are the managing underwriters. In the next layer are syndicate members from the 20 or so "major" firms. More than 70% of the underwriting volume is usually managed by just seven of these majors. Names, reported by Securities Data Co., change from year to year, except for the core of the group—the firms of Morgan Stanley, First Boston, and Goldman Sachs.* None of the investment bankers consistently in this small group of the brains has a significant retail sales force, except Merrill Lynch. What they do have is a reputation for being able to design and manage corporate finance transactions.

If the brawn—the big retail firms like Shearson (American Express), Dean Witter (Sears Roebuck), and Prudential—can ever convince corporate management that they also have the brains, then they could muscle their way to the top of the pyramid. Instead, the brains developed a method to assert their dominance without adding a sales force. They found they could put together a small group of institutional buyers for a new issue of securities, then go to the corporation with a prepackaged underwriting. It was a technique used in Europe called the "bought deal."

"Bought Deals" Replace the Syndicate

Underwritings have been the last of the old fixed-fee businesses to go. One of the ways to remain in everyone else's syndicate is to maintain the industry standard for underwriting fees—6 to 8% for IPOs, depending on the offering size. When there is no syndicate, underwriting fees are at

---

*Three others who have been included for at least the last 20 years are Merrill Lynch, Salomon Brothers and Lehman Brothers. The seventh major position has rotated among Bear Stearns, Dean Witter, Kidder Peabody, PaineWebber and Prudential.

least a full percentage point lower. Since most of the stock is bought by institutions anyway, even with a syndicate, why should a corporate issuer pay extra?

Beginning in 1982, the Securities Exchange Commission (SEC) allowed large corporations to register an offering before picking an underwriter. That let these businesses put the offering on the shelf until an underwriter came to them with a price for the entire issue—a bought deal. These shelf offerings did not allow time for an underwriting syndicate to be put together. The investment banker either presold all the securities to institutional money managers, or took some risk by using its own money to buy for resale.

Back in 1981, the year before the SEC rule was adopted, all but 2% of new common stock issues were sold through syndicates. The next year, more than 30% of the dollar volume was handled entirely by managing underwriters, without an underwriting syndicate. Even an AT&T common stock issue of more than $100 million was all sold by Morgan Stanley to institutional money managers in 1982. This was a dramatic example of how bought deals have replaced syndicated sales to individuals. "Ma Bell' was the symbol of individual shareownership in America—the favorite stock investment of more than two million households. With its huge capital needs, AT&T had been a sustaining source of syndicate fees for retail brokerage firms.

Bought deals have helped the brains do without the brawn. One result has been a drastic reduction in the ranks of brokerage houses that have a retail sales force but no corps of investment bankers on staff.

"Soft Dollar" Orders Replace Syndicate Sales

Just as the issuers of corporate shares chipped away at underwriting fees through inviting bought deals, the institutional money mangers have undermined Wall Street's profits with their own tool—"soft dollars." This device rebates a portion of the underwriting fees by providing research reports and other services "free" to the money manager who places an order for shares.

The mechanics work like this: (1) a money manager decides to invest in shares being sold through an underwriting syndicate, (2) a "research" securities firm has furnished the money manager with research reports, without charge, (3) the money manager orders the shares from the managing underwriter, directing that credit for the sale go to the research firm, and (4) the research firm gets paid 60% of the underwriting fees on those shares. Soft dollars have become big business, with some brokers acting as an exchange—purchasing services for cash from nonbroker vendors and trading them to money managers for commission business.

Now that institutional trading commissions are negotiated, there is little need for soft dollars on stock market transactions. Volume discounts are out in the open. Where the soft dollar business really flourishes is in underwritten new issues—that is the last part of the securities business in which commissions are the same percentage on large orders as on small ones.

Soft dollar deals are a major reason that investment bankers would rather not form a syndicate. If the new issue will be popular with institutions, then make them buy it from the managing underwriter, who can keep the 60% selling portion of the underwriting fee. Forming a syndicate only siphons off commissions through directed orders used to repay soft dollar arrangements.

THERE IS LESS PROFIT
IN SYNDICATED IPOs

One of the reasons so few corporations are going public is that syndicated IPOs appear no longer to be where the money is in investment banking. On a $10 million IPO, with an 8% commission, 80% goes to the selling brokers and for expenses. The managing underwriter stands to collect only $160,000 for investment banking services. Corporate finance departments of Wall Street firms are expected to pay their investment bankers an average of nearly $1 million a year. With the cost of support staff and overhead, they need to generate annual fees of at least $2 million each.

IPOs are very time intensive. A lot of handholding is required, because an IPO involves the financial security and personal dreams of an entrepreneur, who is probably going through this for the first time. Regulatory compliance is often difficult the first time. So is educating the sales department. A new product has to be introduced to the market. Moreover, not every IPO gets done. Some fall out near the end of the process, after most of the time and money has been spent. The successful ones have to carry the cost of the failures.

Most important today is the "opportunity cost" of committing investment bankers to syndicated IPOs. Even a smooth underwriting can use 20% of an investment banker's time over the six-month process. If people are off doing an IPO, they are lost to far more profitable opportunities. For these reasons, more profit is seen in merchant banking, financial engineering, and program trading than in syndicated IPOs.

There Is More Profit in Merchant Banking

Underwriters arrange for money to flow from those who want to invest it to those who want to use it. In merchant banking, the people who do the arranging also put up the money. In addition to a commission, they are in for whatever gain or loss comes from the investment. Morgan Stanley's chairman, S. Parker Gilbert, put it bluntly in his firm's Annual Report for 1988, remarking, "We're becoming a merchant bank, with the whole range of principal activities much more important to us in terms of profits."

There Is More Profit in Financial Engineering

Designing a new security allows a firm to charge fees without any direct competition—until the innovation gets copied. Examples have included "stripping" bonds into separate interest and principal segments and naming them

TIGERS and LIONS; packaging auto loans like bonds and calling them CARS; even attempting an Unbundled Stock Unit to replace common stock.

There Is More Profit in Program Trading

Using proprietary computer software, developed by its in-house "rocket scientists," firms take advantage of momentary price discrepancies between such markets as the stock exchange and stock options. This is seen as a far more profitable use of brains and capital than selling advice for a percentage fee.

HOLLOWING OUT THE MIDDLE
OF THE SYNDICATE

Transformation at the top of the syndicate has drawn away the brains—the investment bankers who brought in the corporate clients and put the stock underwriting together. At the same time, the brawn of underwriting syndicates has been hollowed out—brokerage firms that served individuals have mostly disappeared.

The Vanishing Submajors

Below the 20 or so majors in an IPO tombstone ad, there was once a layer of smaller Wall Street brokerages, the sub-majors. Many of them had investment bankers who could manage IPOs, as well as a staff of retail stockbrokers who brought distribution power to underwriting syndicates.

Samuel Hayes, investment banking professor at Harvard, counted 23 submajor bracket firms for his March-April 1971 *Harvard Business Review* article, "Investment Banking: Power Structure in Flux." These were all important Wall Street presences in the industry and many had national retail networks. By 1978, the list had only two submajors. Five had moved up the pyramid and the other 16 were gone. In his January-February, 1979 *Harvard*

Business Review article, "The Transformation of Investment Banking," Professor Hayes observed that: "The sub-major bracket, which historically provided the vital retail distribution capacity for an underwriting syndicate, . . . has virtually disappeared as a result of the waves of mergers and liquidations in the industry."

There are Fewer Regional Syndicate Members

Brokerage firms with headquarters off Wall Street often had the best retail distribution. They did very little business with institutions and concentrated on using local offices and hometown brokers to serve individuals. The fate of regional firms is illustrated by a comparison with a 1955 tombstone ad, showing syndicate members for a General Motors stock offering. By 1977, every one of the 8 Boston members had gone out of business, as well as 17 of the 24 California firms, and 23 of the 33 in Pennsylvania.

Most of the industry's contraction continues to occur off Wall Street, as regional brokerage firms are acquired or liquidated. At least 15 succumbed during 1988. Many of those remaining have been acquired by financial conglomerates looking for distribution of their life insurance and mutual fund products.

CRUMBLING AT THE BASE
OF THE SYNDICATE

Underwriting syndicates cannot sell a stock issue to individual investors without a broad base of sales people—sales people who have customers interested in buying IPOs. The entire marketing effort is done in two weeks of telephone calls, with no advertising or other supporting communications. So many shares have to be sold, within such a short time, that it is rare for any single firm to do retail stock offerings in-house.

Most damaging to the IPO distribution pyramid has been shrinkage in the sales force. From more than 100,000 brokers in the 1960s, licensed registered representatives at securities firms had dropped below 40,000 by 1977. While that number worked its way back up to 70,000 ten years later, more of the licenses were used to sell products other than corporate shares.

Fewer Securities Analysts Cover Fewer Stocks

The loss of stockbrokers dealing with individuals was not the only damage to those troops needed to sustain under-written IPOs. Also important at the base of the syndicate are the securities analysts who issue reports on industries and individual companies. They generate trading activity in stocks the syndicate has brought to market.

Membership in the New York Society of Security Analysts (NYSSA) began a steep decline in the 1970s. Because of the demise of many regional firms, the NYSSA includes nearly all the brokerage firms' analysts. More important than the decline in the number of analysts is the fact that almost none of them follow corporations that have recently gone public. Why? Because they feel that that is not where the money is. Although there are more than 10,000 stocks being publicly traded, these analysts cover only about 400 of them. Those are the stocks bought and sold by institutional money managers. They are also the stocks for which speculation in stock options is available.

One of Wall Street's rules is that everyone's salary and bonus must be covered by the customers or by the market. High-priced general overhead is not acceptable. That goes for analysts, whose work is either for institutional customers, who will pay soft dollars to document their investment decisions, or for the firm's traders, who try to make money by knowing something before others do. Neither institutional investors nor the firm's traders have an interest in the shares of recent IPOs.

"The Old-Time Stockbroker's a Dying Breed"

John Spooner, the broker who said that to Tim Larrington for his September 20, 1983 *Wall Street Journal* article, explained that "We're becoming an industry of tax shelters and packaged products." There are not many tax shelters anymore, but there are certainly packaged products. And packaged relationships are replacing the one-to-one dialogue of stockbroker and customer.

In the days when syndicates worked better, the power came from thousands of individual brokers, each with a book of customers. Brokers knew their customers' financial situations and personal objectives. When a new offering was announced, these brokers could each call a few likely buyers, talk about the company, and help make a decision.

The retail brokerage house was once a provider of "back office" services to a confederation of independent brokers. These confederations made less sense when brokers no longer owned the place where they worked. In the 1970s, securities firms took themselves public. Others, like Sears, GE, Prudential, and American Express, have since been acquired by huge conglomerates. When a brokerage is a public company, or a corporate division, the objective is net profit and cash flow for the owners. How well the sales force is serviced, or how much the brokers make, is incidental to the bottom line.

The old-time brokers represent a threat to these firms. If they leave, with their book of customers, there is that much less commission business to cover office rent, telecommunications, computers, and support services. Profit for the house is not in being the back office to a group of perceived prima donnas who can storm out the door with their revenue base at any time.

Profit is in capturing customer money and putting it into securities that are manufactured and maintained in-house. Profit is in customers who have turned their money over to the firm for management, without any ties to a particular broker. The way it works was described for James A. White, the author of a March 1, 1990 *Wall Street Journal* article by James D. Awad, president of BMI Capital, which manages client accounts for brokerage firms. "With the managed account business, the broker only has to make a one-time sale to the client, which is a much higher-profit business than trying to sell the client every time the broker comes up with a stock."

PROFIT IN SELLING STOCKS FOR COMMISSIONS HAS DIMINISHED

Commissions on selling stocks and bonds were once nearly the sole source of revenue for the securities industry. Today, commissions are less than 20% of total revenues. And a large portion of those commissions comes from selling futures, options, and other new financial instruments.

As the securities industry shifts away from commissions on stock and bond sales, there are fewer brokers and analysts paying attention to individual corporate shares. Less dialogue takes place with customers about company operations, products, and management. Brokers use IPOs as the subject for cold calling prospects less often. There is not enough profit for the brokerage firm in selling stocks for commissions. Brokers are expected to produce more revenue than they can generate by selling a product that will be held for several years before it is resold. They need the faster turnover provided by futures and options. Brokers are also pushed away from selling individual stocks and toward products that make more money for their employer.

Evergreen Income Is Replacing Commissions

Wall Street is dismantling its commissioned intermediary business and turning to more profitable activities. Today's game plan for individual investors calls for converting them into sources of "evergreen income," a term that describes the year-round flow of fees from the customer, without any repeated selling efforts. Emphasis is away from commissions on transactions and toward getting an annual percentage of the household's assets—these fees come in on a regular basis, so long as the customer's money stays with the firm.

Fees based on assets under management are predictable. They get spread evenly over all four quarters of the year. They do not depend on market cycles or on the personality of particular brokers. Compared with commissions on sales, asset-based fees are ideal for managers. The retail securities business can be made to fit within the financial conglomerates that have replaced Wall Street's producer/ partnerships.

To implement the evergreen income strategy, sales people are encouraged to gather assets through CDs, money market funds, or whatever "bridge" products will attract a customer to do business with the firm. Then the job is to convert that money into something that generates income for the firm just by being there, such as an in-house mutual fund. A major tactic is the "wrap account," which covers both a management fee and brokerage commissions for a flat 3% per year on the customer's assets.

Initial commissions may be unprofitable, as they usually are with brokered CDs or money market funds. But the broker shares in the annual fees from mutual funds or other management by the firm. Gathering assets can provide a stream of future income, with little or no future servicing of the customer. Brokers become new business developers, rather than ongoing advisers.

At a big retailer like Shearson, evergreen fees account for a fourth to a third of total earnings. The firm is much less dependent on commissions generated by a broker's book of customers. And, if the broker leaves, the customers will probably stay.

John Steffens, president of Consumer Markets for Merrill Lynch, described for the September 18, 1988 issue of *Insight* magazine the change from a commission business to evergreen income:

It's called asset gathering. We asked ourselves, "Where are the biggest pools of assets?" The answers were the $2 trillion held in certificates of deposit, several trillion in cash values in insurance policies, a trillion in trusts and a trillion in employee benefit plans. We decided we wanted to gather and manage those assets over a period of time.

One of the more subtle effects of the evergreen strategy is to transfer the judgment-and-trust relationship from the personal broker to the impersonal firm. Stockbrokers who generate commissions by advising customers to buy or sell are disappearing. That leaves no one who can call a few close customers and place shares in an IPO.

Shareowers Are being Switched to Other Products

The NYSE found, in one of its surveys of U. S. shareownership, that most people acquiring stock for the first time had bought shares directly, from employers, rather than through brokers. These newcomers were viewed as prospects for other products. As the NYSE chairman William M. Batten told the 1983 convention of the Securities Industry Association (SIA):

> The essential news, quite obviously, is that the securities industry's customer base has expanded by a whopping 10 million individuals, including 7 million relatively affluent, mostly younger people who have never owned stocks before.
>
> It is probably safe to assume, too, that most of these new customers and prospective customers still do not know very much about such relatively new components of securities firms' product mixes as options and futures.

The logical consequence of this view is for the securities industry to encourage individuals to sell their employer's shares, in order to put the money into products generating evergreen fee income.

INDIVIDUALS FEAR WALL STREET, STOCKS, AND IPOs

Even if the syndicate were to be revitalized somehow, there is another, larger obstacle. Individuals are afraid to do business with Wall Street, afraid to own corporate shares, and afraid of underwritten IPOs. For instance, the surveys of shareowners published periodically by the NYSE show that the number of individual shareowners in the United States grew rapidly, from 6 million in 1952 to 30 million in 1970. Then it dropped to 25 million by 1975. When it began to grow again, it was mostly through employee stock plans, not brokerage accounts. Also, trades of less than 900 shares, typical of individuals, comprised more than 40% of NYSE volume in 1974. Their share was less than 10% ten years later. The volume represented by 100-share orders, a sign of the small investor, fell from 10% to less than 2% in the same decade. According to a survey by the Roper Organization reported in the September 25, 1989 *Wall Street Journal*, only one in five American households holds stocks directly or through a mutual fund, while two out of three holds certificates of deposit. Just 11% said they would trust a stockholder to give good advice on investing a $10,000 windfall, while 35% would trust a commercial bank and 25% would trust a savings and loan. Only 1 in 7 households had dealt with a stockbroker in the past year.

Individuals Are Going to Discount Brokers

Individuals who do buy stocks, based on their own information and judgment, more often use discount brokers—not the firms that are in underwriting syndicates. The discount business concept is a no-frills order execution service: "You call us, we don't call you." It is the exact opposite of telephone selling of underwritten IPOs.

Discount brokers have grown rapidly since they became legitimate in 1975. Estimates of their share of all retail commissions run from only 8 to 10%. However, retail commissions include fees paid for all kinds of brokered transactions: CDs, mutual funds, futures, options, bonds, as well as stocks. Most of the activity is in securities other than corporate shares, especially at full-service firms, where customers are paying for management and advice.

Measured by retail accounts opened, discount brokers pick up about 40% of the new individual investor business each year. These people are choosing to connect with the stock market through brokers who never get invited into underwriting syndicates.

Individuals Are Afraid to Buy Stocks from Brokers

Then there are the individuals who just do not want to do business with a telephone sales broker either because of their past experience or stories they have heard. In a 1986 Harris Poll, 83% of those surveyed said they believe the stock market is driven by "unmitigated greed." Wall Street insiders often confirm this perception.

A warning of these consequences came from Robert Haack, the president of the NYSE, in a speech to the Economic Club on November 17, 1970 in New York, when he said, "Bluntly stated, the securities industry, more than any other industry in America, engages in mazes of blatant gimmickry . . . tending to undermine the entire moral fabric." As the 1990s began, Wall Street was increasingly being portrayed in news, books, and films as dangerous to one's financial health.

Underwritten IPOs Have Mostly Been Poor Investments

1987 was a bad year for most stocks, and only one in five of the IPOs that year was selling at year-end above its offering price. It was worse at the end of 1973, when year-end prices were higher for only 36 of the 417 stocks brought public in the preceding 18 months. Viewing a longer period still shows dismal results.

Some 2,800 IPOs were followed by *Forbes* from 1975 to 1984. Only four in ten showed a higher trading market in late 1985 than the original offering price. Someone buying shares in each offering would have had an overall return of only 3% a year. A December 2, 1985 *Forbes* article asked:

> But wasn't the game worth playing on the chance that you might end up with one of a handful of big winners? Not necessarily. It is unlikely that the average investor could buy 100 shares on the offering of a so-called hot issue because the allocations usually go to favored customers, which often include hedge funds and other institutional investors. So, even if you bought a big winner, chances are you didn't get much of it. Not enough to compensate for the inevitable losers.

University of Illinois professor of finance Jay Ritter did a similar study of 1,526 IPOs during the same decade, summarized in the June 19, 1989 "Your Money Matters" column of the *Wall Street Journal.* The total return on those stocks, including dividends and price changes, was ten percentage points behind Standard & Poor's 500 Index (S&P 500), which comprises large, seasoned corporations.

Ritter also found that favored institutional money managers did much better than the general public. The average IPO stock jumped 14% on the day of the offering, then went back down. Those big investors who "flipped" their new-issue allotment on the first day did very well. Long-term investors did poorly.

Why is the record so poor? According to Alexander Schwartz, co-manager of corporate finance for Prudential-Bache, who was quoted in the March 26, 1984 *Forbes*: "Our industry is totally to blame for encouraging companies to go public that have yet to show profits or have small profits but no real history." Each boom in underwritten IPOs since 1961 has gone bust, driving away thousands of individual investors.

PENNY STOCK BROKERS ARE NOT
THE ANSWER

Since the 1920s, there have always been penny stock brokers. They are the securities firms dealing in corporate shares that come to market for less than a dollar per share. At that price, a customer can invest $10,000 and imagine becoming a millionaire when the share price goes from ten cents to ten dollars.

Some of these brokers run "boiler rooms" or "bucket shops," which have hundreds of licensed representatives making cold calls to prospect lists all over the country. There are wild stories about self-dealing, market manipulation, and other forms of stock fraud. State securities administrators run highly publicized crackdowns, and the games float to a new location. Penny stock brokers will probably always be there. They advertise to entrepreneurs as the way to go public and achieve the American Dream. There may be some who are legitimate. The record of seven decades is against them.

THE CONSEQUENCE: FEW CORPORATIONS
ARE DOING IPOs

The reason why so few corporations are going public is that Wall Street is not making a priority of selling IPOs. At the top of the underwriting syndicate, investment banking brains have deserted IPOs to go into the businesses of merchant banking, program trading, and merger and acquisition (M&A) dealmaking. To protect their position as "majors," they go around the syndicate, arranging bought deals between large corporations and institutional money managers. They are not creating stock offerings for sale to individuals.

The big retail securities houses, the brawn, are paying sales people to put individuals into packaged products; products that generate evergreen income through management fees and rapid turnover. Entrepreneurial stockbrokers, who advise their individual customers on stock selections, are on their way out. Smaller Wall Street firms, the "submajors," are almost gone, as are most of the regional brokerage houses.

There are few signs that Wall Street intends to reverse these trends and return to syndicated IPOs. Even if the securities industry tried to recapture the new-issues booms of the 1960s, Wall Street is no longer likely to be the route to household capital. Individuals are afraid to trust their money to a broker's recommendation. New investors are choosing discount brokers, whose way of doing business does not fit the underwriting syndicate. Nor is there any indication that the securities industry has any other program for matching the supply of household funds with the need for entrepreneurial capital. There will have to be a new market mechanism, and it probably won't come from Wall Street.

CHAPTER 2

The Time Is Right to Market Corporate Shares

Chapter 1 described changes in the securities industry, to show that the reason why so few entrepreneurs are selling shares is that the traditional marketing mechanism is not working very well. It showed that the problem for entrepreneurs in going public could be with the intermediary system, not with the supply of money or the motivation to own shares. Chapter 2 is principally my own opinion about why right now is actually a very good time to be going public. Owning shares in an entrepreneurial corporation fits with some of the major trends—in values, politics, economics, finance, technology, and work—that will be with us for the next several years. Some supporting data and the opinions of others are included in this chapter. There are data which would support contrary conclusions, and several experts who have expressed them. If you are deciding whether to go public, and how to do it, you will make up your own mind. The following are conclusions on each of these trends:

Values: They will likely favor entrepreneurs over bureaucracies. Americans tend not to trust government or big business. We believe in our personal potential and we want a sense of community and participation in decisions affecting our lives.

Politics: It appears to be moving away from geographical boundaries and toward specific issues. One way individuals can regain political power is through corporate shareownership. Control of corporations will likely pass from management bureaucracies to shareowners' parliaments.

Economics: This will likely shift from spending and debt toward savings and investment. It's probable that inflation will continue to subside and interest rates will stabilize at their historic averages. This economic climate would encourage shareownership.

Finance: It will likely break away from Wall Street's control and into direct relationships between corporations and investors. The power of institutional money managers will fade, as will the "casino games" style of speculation they support. Corporate shares will likely return as the favorite financial instrument.

Technology: It will likely make direct communication between individuals and corporations quick and effective. Also likely is that electronic media will permit buying and selling stock to be easy and fair. Through their corporate shares, individuals could own the technology that replaces their labor.

Work: It could lose its class consciousness, as workers become owners. Then, people would work because it follows their own interests, rather than those of managers. Shareownership would free many from dependence on a weekly paycheck.

While some structures are adjusting to meet these changes in attitude and behavior, Wall Street appears to be choosing to concentrate on the past, remaining an intermediary in rearranging and dismantling. The future could be in direct relationships between entrepreneurial corporations and individual investors.

We seem to be coming to the end of bureaucracy as the way to cope with economic realities. Government regulation of business and redistribution of income has not worked very well. Outright government ownership of business has failed and been rejected. What is working are enterprises that meet specific needs and respond quickly to change. In many countries, this occurs in an underground economy. In ours, it is out in the open, but it is burdened by a structure that still accommodates bureaucracies. Change is coming first in the United States. Just as it led the way 200 years ago in political freedom, the United States is forging the paradigm for economic freedom.

THE PARADIGM

In the future, businesses that are patched together around anything but a single objective will lose customers, employees, and access to capital. Corporations will be as large or small as the particular job they are trying to do. Entrepreneurs who lead them may even become heroes and role models, as popular as today's sports and entertainment stars.

Successful corporations could be owned by groups of individuals who have an interest in the business that goes beyond just making money on their investment. These affinity groups will include employees, customers, suppliers, and neighbors. These groups can also arise out of a shared interest in the technology or concept at the core of the corporate purpose. Affinity groups may unite as shareholders internationally, and corporations would lose their national identities. Coalitions will be formed among shareholders of different affinity groups. Corporate parliaments, as alternatives to governmental entities, could enable individuals to carry out their ideas and values.

Shareowners will nominate and campaign for corporate directors with an enthusiasm seldom seen in government elections. Directors will select and monitor chief executive officers for the single purpose of serving the long-term best interests of the shareowners.

Concentration on long-term self-interest will lead to less conflict with the values of the society as a whole. This will allow governments to reduce their role as regulators of business behavior. The politics that most affects our lives will take place in the corporate arena.

Corporations will be an even more important influence on our material world than they are now. But they will be out in the open and subject to the control of vigilant individual shareowners. Corporate behavior will then reflect our current cultural values.

These could be the results of our emerging values, values that can help entrepreneurs market shareownership in their corporations.

WE WANT TO PARTICIPATE IN OUR OWN ISSUES

American structures of business and government have been shaped by cycles of war and economic shocks. Those crises called for mobilization of the whole country under one leader. People had to trust in big hierarchies as the only way to restore peace and prosperity. Few people in business today actually experienced the feelings of panic that characterized the Great Depression, when one in four could not get a job, or World War II, when it was really possible that we could be invaded and conquered. Without those fears, we need not turn our lives over to big government or big business.

Most of our issues today are specific and can best be handled through small organizations that are independent of large bureaucracies. And you and I want to participate in those organizations, to feel we have an influence over their direction and will get our fair share of their results.

In the direct marketing of corporate shares, an entrepreneur is offering a chance to participate—as an owner and a voting member. The corporation will have a specific goal—a human need to meet, a problem to be solved. Shareownership can be offered directly to individuals who have an interest in that goal and want to participate in its achievement.

WE WANT BETTER GAMES TO PLAY

The logical prospects for shareownership are those of us who have some money we do not need to cover basic needs, those of us who can afford to play games. Our old games were merely owning things and looking good. But now we are ready for something more than the creature comforts and the appearance of having made it. We want games that count, that are played out in the real world, and we do not want zero-sum games, where the losses have to match the gains. We are looking for win/win arenas. Personal growth is our challenge.

Investing in corporate shares is a game of skill, as well as chance. Investing is immensely complex, with variables that can never be foreseen. We participate, not only in choosing to buy shares, but also in electing directors and deciding when to sell. We can actually be of service by investing in corporations that meet human needs.

WE WANT TO BE MORE THAN CONSUMERS

Consumer spending reached two-thirds of the gross national product in 1986, in an almost steady rise since 1950. New consumer products and heavy marketing have worked to soak up our income. Then easy consumer credit got us to spend our future earnings.

These are some of the signs that I see: Today, after a few years of declining inflation, we have lost the "buy now before it costs more" fever. We are looking for different ways to feel good. Values from earlier times and other cultures are coming in from the fringe, especially with the increasing power of women and the "60s generation." These post-consumer values open the door to marketing shareownership in entrepreneurial corporations.

Or, take the idea that each generation should consume only the renewable resources of our earth, that we must preserve or replace all that was here. A corporation's products may be directed toward such restoration or preservation. An entrepreneur may have included this value in the way the corporation manufactures its products.

We still want to have things and to look good. Investment in corporate shares will have to pass a rational analysis of risk and reward. It may help if owning particular shares will impress our peers. But corporate shareownership can also be marketed as a way for us to be more than what we consume.

WE WANT TO DO IT OURSELVES

Most of us do not trust others to know what is best for us. So we become informed, the better to use our own judgment. We read the labels for ingredients and warnings. We ask others with experience. Many of us who are already investors use discount brokers. We may belong to one of the 7,000 investment clubs or to an individual investor association. Our sources of information include a business news media that has vastly expanded in the past few years. Scores of investment newsletters and data bases have become available through our PCs. We are smart shoppers—educated and hungry to learn. High pressure, fear-and-greed pitches will not work with us. What will work is a direct communication from an entrepreneur, telling us what the corporation has done and where it is headed. We can then figure out what is in it for us.

WE WANT ADVERTISING TO INFORM US

Advertising and promotion have become our first source of knowledge. Sure, we know it is intended to convince us to buy, but we can separate the facts from the puffery. Advertising is efficient. We skim the newspaper or magazine. A radio or television message only affects us for 30 or 60 seconds. With our mail, we can stop at the envelope, at the peek inside, at the first sentence. We know about public relations, the way advertising is sometimes disguised as news. We take it in with the understanding that we are being sold.

Advertising is entertainment. It is art. We get humor, music and stimulation of our basic drives. Advertising has worked well in helping us to spend on things we use or consume. Advertising will be just as effective in persuading us to invest in corporate shares.

POLITICS

Governments are not working very well. Most of us feel our participation in them will not make any difference in what gets done. Corporate shares can provide us with a place to put our time and money where we can hope it will make a difference.

Corporations Could Replace Governments

For a while, we left all our social problems to the government—assign the issue to the public schools, create a new department, or put another line in the budget. But now we have learned that governments are limited in what they can do. They only seem to work when the issues affect us all in about the same way. One giant lesson has been that government-owned business does not work. Nor does protection of business through regulated prices or territories. Nations that combined business and government are now restructuring their economies.

Privatization has been underway since 1979 in Great Britain, where government-owned industry has declined from 10% of gross domestic product to 6%. More than 50 countries have joined in selling government-owned businesses. Sales prices totaled $43 billion in 1988 alone. In the United States, the trend is to cut business loose from government support, through deregulation and tax reform. Competition among corporations is replacing the government in determining how economic needs will be met. Corporations are becoming more global and less identified with particular nations. This has happened because of world-wide marketing, foreign manufacturing operations and, now, globalized stock markets, which are adding the element of international ownership.

National governments will continue to decline as the instruments for meeting our needs. Perhaps they worked best when war was the ultimate power play. We are now in a world where business and money, not armies and weapons, determine who gets what. Corporations can be the vehicles for getting things done. Ownership of corporate shares can be the way to participate in the process of meeting human needs.

Corporate Parliaments Are Replacing CEO Kingdoms

Owning stock in a big corporation has not provided individuals with any sense of influence or participation. The corporation has been the domain of one person, the chief executive officer (CEO), who selects a board of directors and a line of succession. Although many CEOs claim to serve "multiple constituencies" of suppliers, bank lenders, employees, customers, and the general public, as well as shareholders, legislative proposals to reduce the double tax on dividends were defeated by lobbyists for big corporate managements. These CEOs would rather keep those earnings to increase their realms. Meanwhile, dividends, as a percentage of earnings, are at their lowest level in nine years.

Institutional investors have been forced to break the "Wall Street Rule," which says: "If you do not like what the CEO is doing, vote with your feet—sell the stock." However, the managers of huge public pension funds found they could not do this without taking losses because of their size and the limited number of blue chip corporations in which to invest. These big investors have begun acting like owners—voting against management and making their own proposals, meeting with CEOs to express their sentiments. This is helping to shift power in corporate governance from CEOs to shareowners.

There is an opportunity to market participatory share-ownership, in contrast to maintaining a managerial class that reduces shareholders to the status of depositors. Shareowners can vote by secret ballot. Cumulative voting will allow any substantial coalition of owners to be heard. Directors can be nominated by shareowners and the entrepreneur/CEO can be the only employee allowed to be a director. The board chairman can be a significant share-owner who really runs the board on behalf of the share-owners.

Entrepreneurs Could Replace Bureaucrats

Americans have always preferred small organizations to large ones. We distrust concentrations of power. These feelings have come to be centered on bureaucratic corporations that seem to be responsible only to the person at the top, who is responsible to no one. We admire the individual who ventures out with a small band of followers.

The biggest movement in business is the tearing apart of large corporations. It is as if the question had been asked: "How can we have corporations that are the right size, run by people motivated to serve the shareowners?" And the answer was: "By starting with big bureaucracies, breaking them into rational units and turning them over to people with an owner's motivation." The era of takeover and breakup will run its course, as the supply of bargains declines. Besides, this is a game for only a few big players. The rest of us will get a chance to play a more constructive game—backing entrepreneurs, who can replace bureaucrats.

Individual Shareowners Are Replacing Custodians

For a while in the 1970s, it seemed as if all the corporate stock would be owned by pension funds and insurance companies. Their rate of growth, had it continued, would have soaked up most of the available shares. There was a continuing decline in the number of individuals who were direct owners of corporate shares. The trend has turned around. The percentage of institutional ownership has stopped growing, even as the total amount of stock outstanding has decreased through takeovers and repurchases. Individuals are again becoming direct owners of shares through employee stock purchase programs.

Executives came to realize what payments into pension plans were doing to corporate earnings and cash flow, especially as institutional money managers continued to underperform market averages.

CEOs retreated from defined benefit programs to the more predictable defined contribution method. Many substituted programs in which the employee has to make some of the investment decisions. Others turned to plans that invested in the employer's own stock.

There has been encouragement from Washington for the concept of more individual shareownership. The following is from page 171 of the 1976 Report of the Joint Economic Committee of Congress:

> To begin to diffuse the ownership of capital and to provide an opportunity for citizens of moderate incomes to become owners of capital rather than relying solely on their labor as a source of income and security, the Committee recommends the adoption of a national policy to foster the goal of broadened ownership.

Pension reform is happening in Congress. The 1992 election year may see some restoration of tax incentives for individual ownership of corporate shares. Individual retirement accounts (IRAs) are likely to make a comeback. The political winds are right for marketing corporate shares to individual investors.

ECONOMICS

Most economic factors seem to come and go, and come back again. Individual investing in corporate shares has been that way. It was big in the 1920s and 1950s but has not come around since. In my opinion, there are three economic cycles supporting a return to shareownership in the next few years:

The country is moving from inflation to stable prices,

The country is displacing jobs with technology, and

The country is starting to spend less and save more.

From Inflation to Stable Prices

Inflation has happened over many centuries in different civilizations. It has always ended. And it is during the periods of price stability that individuals have most often purchased corporate shares or an older culture's equivalent.

But *when* will inflation end this time? According to the behavior of money supply and interest rates, price stability is on its way back soon.

There is good news for those who believe that prices increase because there is more money available to spend. "Too much money chasing too few goods." The supply of money has recently been growing at below Federal Reserve target levels. Individuals have less money to spend, because inflation-adjusted wages have gone down during most of the past 15 years and are 8% below 1972 levels. A slowdown in business spending is suggested by the two-year decline in the index of leading indicators.

The interest rate reduction that began in 1982 has survived some relapses and will continue, until we reach the levels that have existed in most of the past few hundred years—2 to 4% for long-term government bonds. Lower interest rates shift money away from fixed-income investments and into corporate shares.

From Jobs to Technology

Unemployment has been a great fear ever since families began migrating from farms to the cities during the 1500s. It has been the theme of religious reformation, political revolution, literature, and the arts. We went through our last round of that awful fear during the Great Depression. Then World War II put people back to work. The war seemed to prove that the answer was to create a demand for goods and services that were quickly used up.

In peacetime, the consumption of war material was replaced by the consumption of household goods and services. We invented consumer products, our advertising told us about them, and our retailers sold them. Jobs were created, incomes rose, we spent more—which meant more jobs and income and spending. There were plenty of jobs available to absorb our increasing population. More money for consumer spending was created when the proportion of women working increased, from about a third in the 1950s to well over half in 1988.

But the spending/jobs/income system developed problems. Inflation sent prices up faster than wages. What we produced, per hour worked, stopped increasing fast enough to let our employers pay us more for doing the same work. Now we have to use technology to extend what humans can do.

Productivity—output per worker—will be to the next few years what the goal of full employment was to the past.

According to *The Economist's* May 27, 1989 issue, "The biggest threat to America's economy is not of a sudden financial heart attack but of a prolonged wasting disease, which erodes the country's productivity and future living standards. Depressingly for Americans, their productivity growth in the 1980s has been the slowest of all the seven largest OECD economies." We spend less than any other major industrialized country on research and development related to industrial growth. Our production of machine tools and other capital goods has just turned upward for the first time in ten years.

We have been making more jobs, rather than better workplace technology, because it has seemed cheaper. The cost of capital—interest rates—has been much higher than before the 1960s, and the cost of labor has either been stable or lower. Those days are over. The study of demographics predicts a decline in the supply of new workers, particularly in the number of women applying for jobs and the number of young people reaching working age.

The future will be for those who can finance new production technology through marketing shares, rather than by borrowing money. Financing new tools through borrowed money, the route big corporations would likely take, means paying interest and setting aside cash for repayment. Shareowner capital is the natural way to match the risk and reward potential of investing in tools.

Entrepreneurs have a huge advantage over bureaucratic corporations in their cost of shareowner capital. Big corporations will have to sell stock at the price of their shares in the trading market, usually in the range of 10 to 15 times current earnings. Entrepreneurs can generally offer shares at higher multiples of current earnings. Investors see a greater chance of rapid growth and increased earnings from young companies than from mature corporations. But this advantage is academic with underwritten stock offerings. Institutions are the stock buyers in an underwriting, and they mostly want big companies. To get long-term investors, investors willing to take the risk of delay and failure, shares must be marketed to individuals.

From Spending to Investing

Spending was our national policy for more than 50 years. Spending brought production and production meant jobs. So we taxed away savings, gave tax deductions for borrowings, and encouraged spending on things that were quickly used up and left a demand for more.

But what about when we spent on things produced outside the United States? What about when foreign producers invested in tools that would increase production without having to hire more people? What happened to this spending policy when other countries caught up with our ability to produce? What happened was that those countries increased wages, improved quality, and reduced costs—all at once. They had policies that discouraged spending and funneled money into building tools for production. We were stuck with tax laws and government programs that made it difficult to keep markets or increase incomes.

Change at the talk level began more than ten years ago. By the end of 1990, there had been consistent growth in the acceptance of the need to spend less and invest more. Change at the action level in government was finally underway. Deductions for interest on consumer debt had largely been eliminated. The tax rate on investment income had been lowered. Direct government spending programs were continuing to shrink. Even the defense budget was beginning to decline, following reductions in other countries.

While these trends will be interrupted by the war with Iraq and the recession, government spending had not been the culprit in the past few years before 1991. It increased by just 1% of national income, from 22.8% to 23.8%, between the 1970s and the 1985-87 period. But individual consumption was up five points in the same period, from 69.3% to 74.1% of national income. Savings—the percentage of our national income left over after spending—was 7% to 8% in the 1970s and 2% to 4% in the mid-1980s. Since investment comes from savings, net investment in business fell from 7% of gross national product in the 1970s to less than 5% in the mid-1980s.

Thus, if we start spending less, we save more and there is more money for investing in corporate shares. Can we spend less? Will we choose to spend rather than save, or do we need to use 98% of our national income just to get by?

There are both signs and reasons showing that the spending/saving cycle has reached its spending apogee and is on the way back toward an increase in money available for buying corporate shares. For instance, the personal savings share of after-tax income went from 3.2% in 1987 to 4.2% in 1988 and was in the 5 to 6% range during 1989 and 1990. That translates into $100 billion more per year available, which could be invested in shares. Also, of the 3.6% increase in the consumption-to-income ratio between 1981 and 1987, 3.5% was for discretionary purchases, not necessities. Moreover, consumer installment credit, which went from 7% of disposable income in 1950 to 19% in 1987, has been level for the last two years. Lastly, car loans, which make up 40% of consumer credit, now have an average maturity of 4.7 years. Many have balances of more than the car's trade-in value, slowing new car sales.

On average nationally, we have started to spend less, and many of us can afford to spend a lot less. Nearly 30% of American households have "discretionary income," which the Census Bureau defines as money left over after taxes and the necessities of life. That translates into 26 million households in the United States that have an average discretionary income of $12,300—at total of $319 billion a year.

It is true that our spending is still a huge percentage of our national income. But the statistics average together all American households. Some of us spend all of this year's income and part of next, using five-year car loans and increasing credit card balances. Since some of us are spending more than 100% of our income, that means that others of us are saving at way beyond the income-minus-spending average. Even within the same household, it is not inconsistent for us to borrow at cheap car loan rates and also invest in corporate shares. While consumer debt is high, households receive far more interest income, on deposits and other lender instruments, than they pay in interest expense.

Individuals have an immense amount of money already set aside, money that could be used for buying shares. Our deposits just in savings institutions have grown from $11 billion in 1950 to nearly $900 billion today. Bank deposits, real estate equities, mutual funds—all reflect our decisions to save and invest.

FINANCE

Values, politics, and economics have coalesced at this time, creating a matrix in which entrepreneurs can raise capital. That means the right financial technique is the direct marketing of corporate shares to individual investors.

Corporate Shares Are the Best Financial Instrument

We have come through a period in which earning interest looked better than owning shares. It was also a time when tax laws, inflation, and institutional investors combined to chill individuals' interest in stocks. That tide has turned. Before 1958, dividends on corporate shares provided a better current income than interest on deposits or bonds. Since then, there has been a "reverse yield." Dividends, as a percentage of stock prices, have been less than interest, as a percentage of bond prices. That explains very simply why the number of shareowners increased by 250% in the 15 years through 1958 and why individuals have been selling stocks ever since.

Throughout history, stock yields have been lower than bond yields only 2% of the time. Yet, a reverse yield has been the norm for the past 30 years. Stock yields have been relatively steady—in the 3 to 5.5% range. The reverse-yield phenomenon has been a function of interest rates, which historically are from 2 to 4% on deposits and top-quality bonds.

As interest rates continue to decline, individuals will return to buying corporate shares, the way they did in the 1950s.

Deposits. Interest rates on insured deposits are likely to decrease even faster than on bonds. Capital ratio regulations encourage banks to reduce assets and deposits. Instead of holding on to the loans they make, banks are packaging them as securities, for sale to institutional investors. The banks can then let deposits flow out by cutting the rates they pay individuals.

Government Bonds. These public debt obligations will soak up far less money in the future. Britain has been running a budget surplus since fiscal 1987. Japan's deficits peaked in 1983 and surpluses are expected by 1991. United States' deficits have been falling as a percentage of gross national product since 1985 and could be gone by the mid-1990s.

Corporate Bonds. Long-term corporate debt instruments are not likely to attract more money from individuals, for they are very different from the simple IOUs issued by the government. Corporate debt instruments involve indentures and covenants and trustees. An investor in such long-term instruments needs to research the fine print of 100-page legal documents, as well as the credit of the company. Directors and managers have a legal duty to shareowners—to do everything to protect and enrich them that they would do for themselves. Their duties to bondholders are limited to what is in the legal documents.

Junk Bonds. Disillusion with corporate bonds will increase because of the junk bond experiences. There are $200 billion of these high-yield, high-risk debt instruments outstanding, compared with only $2 billion ten years ago. They do not carry investment grade credit ratings from Moody's or Standard & Poor's, so most investors have had to trust the investment bank that sold them the bonds.

Junk bonds became acceptable because investors bought two assumptions: (1) the investment bank that sold them the bonds would always make a market—there would always be an offer to buy them back—and (2) if the bond issuer got in trouble, the investment bank would find a way to refinance and prevent a default. Both of the assumptions were proved mistaken in 1989. In the first nine months of the year, 14 companies had defaulted on $3.4 billion in junk bonds. Several major junk bond investment bankers refused to make offers, at any price, to buy back bonds they had initially sold.

Options and Futures. At the riskier end of the investment spectrum, the options and futures market scandals have generated plenty of publicity for the fact that individuals nearly always come out behind. These are zero-sum games, in which there is an equal loss for every gain. Commissions on the frequent turnover can quickly eat up any profits.

Limited Partnerships.　We can expect less money to flow into limited partnerships. They are a cumbersome alternative to corporate shares, used to pass through tax losses and avoid the corporate double tax on dividend income. Congress has wiped out most of those advantages.

Miserable performance should help end the era of limited partnership investing. Some 12 million individuals put $100 billion into limited partnerships over the past decade. Their losses are estimated at $24 billion. Now they are learning that getting out of limited partnership investments is nothing like the trading market for corporate shares. Selling can be slow, difficult, and costly.

Sales of real estate limited partnerships have gone down from $8.4 billion in 1986 to a $2.3 billion annual rate in 1989. That drop comes despite rich incentives for the securities industry—selling commissions of 8%, as well as other fees that bring total front-end costs to 15%—plus annual management charges.

Mutual Funds.　There are more than a thousand stock mutual funds today, four times as many as ten years ago. As they have grown larger, their performance has grown worse. In the five years through 1989, only 37% of all diversified U.S. stock funds did as well as the S&P 500, down from 52% in the previous five years. These results are not encouraging more individuals to invest in funds.

These managed investment pools will probably always have their place. But they do not work for those of us who want to participate in selecting particular businesses, in voting shares, or communicating with management. If professional managers do worse than a dart board or other random selection, it does not really cost us to play the game ourselves.

The Supply of Shares Has Been Decreasing

Individuals have been receiving cash in the redemption or takeover of shares in amounts far in excess of their new share purchases. According to the Federal Reserve, the supply of shares decreased by $287 billion in the 1985-88 period. The ownership of corporate shares by households was reduced even more, by $401 billion during those four years, as mutual funds and foreigners increased their shareholdings.

Most of this shift away from corporate shares occurred not because individuals chose to sell. Buyouts by private groups and repurchases ordered by management forced investors to exchange shares for cash. Harvard professor Jay Light, in the September-October *Harvard Business Review,* has estimated that, if the trend continues, "the last share of common stock owned by an individual will be sold in the year 2003." Experience shows that the trend will probably not continue that long—that the cycle will come around and individuals will buy corporate shares.

Meanwhile, there is a plentiful supply of money going into other financial instruments. In 1988, when a net $96 million of corporate shares were removed from public ownership, the amount of deposits increased by $198 million, while net purchases of government and corporate bonds totaled $457 billion.

When corporate shares are once again marketed to individuals, the supply of money will be there. Historically, the only channel for marketing new shares has been underwritten IPOs through investment bankers. The bankers have abandoned that activity in the past few years, largely to earn fees in the takeovers and restructurings that have reduced the supply of shares. Direct marketing will enable entrepreneurs to reverse this flow and recapture the billions that have come out of individual shareownership.

"Deleveraging" Has Already Begun

While corporations have been taking shares out of investors' hands, they have had to increase corporate debt. Total corporate liabilities have gone from 45% of gross national product in 1980 to 54% in 1989. There are signs that the tide has turned, that stock will now begin replacing debt. Some of the biggest corporate users of junk bonds and other debt are beginning the process of "deleveraging," paying off those liabilities from money obtained through issuing shares.

There are many explanations for the reversal. Junk bonds now cost a 7% premium over Treasury bonds, compared with just 2% a few years ago. The stock market has become more favorable, with higher price-earnings (P/E) ratios. Maybe it is simply the cycle that swings between net stock redemptions and net stock issuances.

Selling Shares Could Be an Entrepreneur's Best Alternative

Entrepreneurs with big-league dreams will reach a point where growth outstrips available capital. Selling shares to the public allows an entrepreneur to get the necessary money and still keep control of the business. With the underwritten IPO market largely unavailable to them, what have entrepreneurs been doing as they reach the going public stage? Thousands of them have been selling out.

Selling Out. The number of companies merged or acquired, in the $3 to $100 million price range, has gradually increased from 13,500 in 1985 to an estimated 18,500 in 1989. Their large competitors bought them to increase market share. Foreign buyers used them to enter U.S. markets. Many an entrepreneur has cashed out well, but no longer had a business to build.

Venture Capital. An alternative to selling the whole business is to negotiate a private investment. The traditional source, venture capital firms, have received most of their money during the past few years from institutional investors. As a result, many of them have become bureaucracies, protecting jobs by avoiding risk and by tying up entrepreneurs in a maze of restrictions.

When there is no functioning IPO market, the character of the venture capital market is changed as well. Any investor has to have an exit plan or two. Going public was the best one for successful venture investments. Now, the plan has to contemplate forcing the entrepreneur to sell out.

Institutional Investors. Institutions have lots of money. But very little of it has flowed directly into shares of entrepreneurial corporations. Institutional structures only seem to accommodate corporate investments that are channeled through managers and brokers. Insurance companies and some pension funds can put billions into office buildings and shopping centers, using their own in-house staff to evaluate and monitor these investments. No similar process has ever worked well for buying shares of private corporations.

Besides, the great migration of money into pension funds is no longer growing. The hundred largest money managers saw their pension accounts nearly double between 1984 and 1988 to a total of $2 trillion. The private sector side of that growth reversed in 1988, when corporate pension funds paid out $10 billion more in benefits than they received in new money. Funds for government employees are still growing, but about 80% of U. S. pension plans are overfunded, with $300 billion more than they are expected to need to pay benefits. This trend will accelerate, as employers move away from defined benefit plans, install employee stock purchase programs, allow employees to direct their own pension investments, and shift from having employees to contracting jobs.

The trend is that institutions will increasingly invest only in the stocks of very large companies. But it will probably be less and less through professional managers, who are paid a fee to pick individual stocks. Their results have been worse than the stock market averages. So those responsible for the funds will likely shift to indexing, using a computer-based program for investing throughout the entire market for acceptable stocks. Indexing keeps a weighted dollar amount in each corporation's shares. As the stock market averages go, so goes the fund's portfolio.

Indexing will soak up shares in the 200 to 1,000 major corporations. They will become the "institutional market." Any employer that still tries management of a pension fund through stock picking will be playing with money that is there for employees and retirees.

As institutions take over the big corporation stock market, entrepreneurs and individuals are becoming free to develop their own markets.

Individual Shareownership Is a Worldwide Trend

An announced motive for privatization—selling shares of government-owned businesses to individuals—has been to create "a nation of shareholders." Former Prime Minister Margaret Thatcher has said: "It should be as natural for people to own shares as to own their own home or car." French government television commercials promote: "Shares—Today's Way to Save." Factories in Eastern Europe are selling shares to their workers. Managers want to sell stock to the public, to make use of money earned in the black market. Russian co-ops, which are like limited partnerships, may soon be permitted to become corporations. They have increased 600% in number in the past year, to 100,000, and their revenues have grown much faster. Stock exchanges are blossoming in many European and Southeast Asian nations, attracting investment from local residents and from all around the world.

Direct Share Marketing Is an Established Method

Corporate shares have been marketed directly for many years. The applications have been in special ways, to particular markets, but the direct share marketing method is well established. Employee stock purchases plan, sales to existing shareowners, little-known but available programs for people who are not already shareowners, and informal investing are among the ways shares are now directly marketed.

Employee Stock Purchase Plans.   A majority of the individuals who are investing in stock for the first time are being offered ownership in the shares of their employer. Most of the publicity has concerned employee stock ownership plans (ESOPs) where a bank or other trustee is the legal shareowner and management is motivated by tax benefits or takeover protection. But the trend of legal rules for ESOPs is to pass real ownership on to the employees.

Stock options—the right to buy stock at a favorable price—are being issued to many more employees. In the past, options were for top management only. When the options are exercised, the sale of stock occurs directly between the employer and the employee, without a broker.

Sales to Existing Shareowners.   Through rights offerings, new shares are made available to current shareowners. Corporations are often able to meet all their new equity capital needs through rights offerings. Individuals welcome the chance to increase their investment without paying any brokerage fees.

Dividend reinvestment programs allow shareowners to apply their dividends to buying more shares. First started in 1969, they came to be offered by more than 1,200 corporations, with 6 million shareowners participating. In some years, a quarter of all equity capital raised by public corporations has been through dividend reinvestment.

Corporations have been careful not to offend the securities industry, but that has apparently not been a problem. AT&T, which raised $1.1 billion through dividend reinvestment in 1980, first made a survey of securities brokers before it started its program. According to the company's investor relations manager, Anthony A. Parra, "A great majority [of brokers] said that they were happy we are doing this because we are taking business that is a thorn in their side. They don't make a heck of a lot of money on small orders such as this."

Dividend reinvestment plans were extended gradually. Some companies give discounts of 5% or so from the current market price. Many let shareowners add new cash to the dividend amount. Next came "optional cash investing" programs, in which anyone owning at least one share can buy directly, from the corporation, up to as much as $60,000 at a time. Directories are available that describe the features of each program. There is a service that will funnel an individual's cash into particular plans on a monthly basis.

Sales Programs for People Who Are Not Already Shareowners. Now there are programs open to people who are not shareowners at all. Several corporations will allow an individual to first become a shareowner through a direct investment. These programs are passive—an investor needs to take the initiative to discover where they are available and how to buy shares.

Citicorp took the last step in the logical progression by actively marketing shares directly to people who are not already shareholders. The firm's Citibank subsidiary included with 5 million credit card bills the pitch: "Investors: Now you can buy Citicorp stock directly, no fees, no commissions." In its initial phase, more than 12,500 cardholders bought Citicorp shares by mail. Average investment was $1,200.

"Informal Investing." Entrepreneurs are already marketing shares directly to individuals at an annual rate of $33 billion. This is the so-called informal investing that takes place through little networks across the country. Individuals and entrepreneurs learn about each other through their accountants, their dentists, through friends of friends.

According to "The Informal Supply of Capital," a report submitted January 29, 1988 by Robert J. Gaston and Sharon Bell to the Small Business Administration (SBA), "informal investment appears to be the largest source of external equity capital for small businesses," more than banks and eight times as much as the amount raised from venture capital firms. The SBA studied the informal investments of 435 individuals. They averaged three or four corporate investments, of about $60,000 each. Total participation in the informal investing market for the period 1982-1987 was estimated by the SBA at 445,600 companies and 719,600 investors. The average annual rate of informal investing in corporate shares was $32.7 billion, compared with less than $4 billion by venture capital firms and less than $5 billion in underwritten IPOs. This level of direct investment between entrepreneurs and individuals took place without any direct public marketing. It happened because there is a massive demand and an immense supply—even without a marketing mechanism to bring them together.

TECHNOLOGY

Most corporate shares are still marketed and traded through technology unchanged since the 1920s: Its media are the telephone and the trading floor. The methodology is that of collecting a percentage commission from every transaction. Capital is being allocated by a trading technology and a trading mentality, a combination that tends to cause turnover in existing businesses, rather than bring life to new ones.

The securities industry is a labor-intensive business, with an extremely high unit labor cost. Sustaining its low-tech nature requires big deals or rapid turnover. Wall Street paraphernalia is not the right mechanism for matching entrepreneurs and individuals in long-term shareownership.

New technology is ready. It has been tested. We are entering the stage in which the techniques of direct marketing will create a flow of capital from individual investors to entrepreneurs; telecomputer trading markets will bring liquidity and a sense of fairness to individuals who invest in new shares; and the new capital will finance cybernetics, the technology that replaces human labor, freeing investors from dependence on wages.

The Techniques of Direct Marketing

Going public without an underwriter is a simple progression from the direct marketing of other financial instruments. There is plenty of recent experience in bypassing securities wholesalers and retailers. These techniques include commercial paper, Treasury bills, notes, and bonds, savings deposits, brokers, fundraisers, credit bureaus, and IPOs, which are discussed below.

Commercial Paper. Large corporations sell these IOUs, due in less than nine months, to companies with extra cash on hand. Most of the money exchanged directly between corporate treasurers, through commercial paper, would otherwise have gone into banks as deposits and back out as bank loans.

From less than $5 billion in 1961, commercial paper grew in 20 years to a $100 billion market. There are securities firms that act as commercial paper dealers, but most commercial paper is placed directly by the issuer with the investor.

Treasury Bills, Notes, and Bonds. The U.S. Treasury has built a very successful, low-key direct marketing program for individual investors. At its regular weekly auctions to the securities and banking industries, the Treasury also accepts "noncompetitive bids" of $10,000 or more. Individuals get their Treasury bills, notes, or bonds at the same price as those sold at the auction.

The Department of Treasury has chosen not to advertise its direct sales program. But it has used two other very important direct marketing tools—public relations and customer service.

When a news story mentions the results of a Treasury auction, it will usually refer to the amount of noncompetitive bids. There will often be a sentence or two that tells the reader to ask at any Federal Reserve Bank for information. Occasionally, there will be a feature story about the availability of direct purchases. These public relations seem to be carefully managed in order to get the word out without telling people to short-circuit their bank or broker.

Once we have picked up the idea to buy Treasury bills, notes, and bonds directly, the way has been made very easy. Telephone directories have a special listing under "Federal Reserve Bank" for direct sales. There is an efficient, friendly person to help us, at a clearly designated window at the Federal Reserve Bank. The one-page form is simple, and it can be done through the mail. Interest can be credited directly to our checking account. U.S. savings bonds became available in 1988 through a 24-hour telephone service. Individuals can call 800-US BONDS and pay for investments on their credit cards.

Savings Deposits. Technology in the use of media to promote investment products has had as much inventing and testing as money could buy in the past few years. All the deregulation of financial services has launched a thousand major campaigns. When banks an S&Ls were allowed to compete with money market funds, they sold $100 billion worth of accounts within the first nine months. All the media were used. Every ad agency had its creative department pull out the stops.

Brokers. There have been piecemeal attempts to use some direct marketing techniques within the securities industry—mailed invitations to seminars, interactive video presentations by satellite, pitches on VCR cassettes. They lead to a telephone or in-person closing, but much of the broker's prospecting and "qualifying" work has already been done.

Fundraisers. Direct marketing technology is startling in its ability to select target markets, suggest what motivates them, and find the media to reach them. Some of the most advanced techniques have come from fundraising for political and charitable causes.

Credit Bureaus. There are three major companies (TRW, Equifax, and Trans Union Credit Information) that verify the creditworthiness of people who want to charge their purchases or borrow money. They have records on 160 million Americans. Banks, retailers, and others give the bureaus monthly computer tapes, with the purchases and payments of nearly every household. Other information is added to personal files from driving records, employment histories, and bank balances. Magazines sell subscription lists, mail order firms and charitable fundraisers provide information. All of this is merged and can be sorted to fit a profile of the target market.

IPOs. Going public through direct marketing has been done for many years. Each time, entrepreneurs were largely reinventing the wheel. For instance, Control Data Corporation sold shares door-to-door in 1957. Two years earlier, James Ling took LTV public through a booth at the Texas State Fair. Ads in Vermont newspapers in 1984 gave local residents the chance to buy shares of Ben & Jerry's Homemade Inc., the premium ice cream maker.

Except for the direct IPOs of savings institutions in the early 1980s, there has been no cumulative body of experience from which to design and manage a program. Direct marketing of shareownership is where hamburger stands were before McDonald's, where air courier services were before Federal Express. The market is there. The technology is ready. It only needs systems and commitment.

The Electronic Stock Exchange

With most stock trading, the only information we get comes from the person who is selling us shares, or buying them back. And the only way we can buy or sell is through that broker-dealer. Old technology still dominates trading in corporate shares. Investors can only have access to the market through brokers, who usually deal through specialists and market makers. As a result, it all seems very one-sided—the insiders taking advantage of the outsiders.

The laws are in place for us to get our information and complete our trades on a far more equal footing. Congress mandated a national market system in the Securities Reform Act of 1975. Why does it not happen? Resistance to a fairer, cheaper market comes from those who make money the old way. The SEC considers that its mandate is to protect the securities industry, as well as police it. So the SEC has done virtually nothing to carry out the expressed will of Congress, which would radically change the highly profitable specialist role.

The ease of switching to electronic trading is shown by the path taken by insiders for their own trades. Rule 390 of the NYSE requires all its member brokers to place orders for listed stocks through its specialists, who run around the trading floor with pad and pencil. Many members choose instead to go through a nonmember broker, which does trades of 3,000 shares or less all by computer. It takes 4 seconds and can save $30 on a 1,000 share order.

Extensions of existing software would permit anyone with a computer and modem to have access to all bid-and-ask quotes, trading history, and published information on any public corporation. Buy-and-sell orders could be executed directly.

The SEC has also been dragging its feet on making information about public companies retrievable by personal computers. With them, individuals could readily get the information now funneled through stockbrokers and investment advisers. For years, it has been assigning low priority to Electronic Data Gathering, Analysis and Retrieval (EDGAR) and has set 1993 for requiring electronic filings from 11,000 publicly traded companies.

Technology is already in place to take stock trading and investment analysis from the trading post to the computer terminal. There are 24 million personal computer (PC) users in the United States. That is just counting homes and small businesses. More than half of our affluent households have computers. Software is marketed, some by discount brokers, that allows information retrieval, investment analysis, and stock trading to be done entirely by telecomputing—no human voice necessary. Corporations can have the full text of their news releases available within 15 minutes to anyone with a terminal and modem. For $8 a month, a subscriber can have releases on companies and industries automatically put into a PC memory.

When trades and information go through a telecomputer system, monitoring for unlawful behavior becomes much more effective. Investors then feel less dependent upon market professionals.

Cybernetics Could Be the New Economic Engine

As used in the description of trends in technology, cybernetics means the use of machines and computer programs to replace tasks now performed by humans, especially those involving the five human senses and logical thought processes.

Cybernetics is synthetic human energy and synthetic mental processing. It performs the basic recognition of our senses, the matching with patterns in our memories, and the instructing of body parts to move in certain ways. Synthetic human energy comes from electricity, which will become far more plentiful and less expensive, as we make strides in such technologies as photovoltaics and superconductivity.

It's likely that synthetic mental processing will come from increasing speed and storage capacity in computer hardware, which allows for more complex programming. Simple, single-purpose computer chips, which replace many human functions, are already used in assembly line manufacturing. Entrepreneurs will bring forth applications beyond our imaginations.

Technological breakthroughs have catapulted us into long cycles of growth. We are entering such a period now, one that can bring the kind of economic activity that followed the invention of the steam engine and the automobile—a cycle that can improve our standard of living the way it was changed by the electric motor and the transistor/microchip.

That technological breakthrough will likely come in cybernetics, the computer/communications/mechanical systems that can do the tasks humans now perform. Tools can liberate our bodies and minds from having to produce and maintain. Ownership of those tools, through corporate shares, could be marketed to individuals. Dividends and trades in shares could replace some of the income we now receive in wages. The market for shares in entrepreneurial corporations may expand as individuals come to believe that they could achieve the American dream. For most of us, that would be doing what we want with our time, while still having enough income to meet our needs and primary wants.

With inexpensive and inexhaustible electrical energy, it could become feasible to desalinate water and move it anywhere. Combustible fuels can be produced from renewable resources through safe processes. We will remove the economic limits on using motors, heating, and cooling.

Capital for these entrepreneurs will come from individuals, from people who share the vision and have enough faith to take a risk. When a venture hits, it will bring its shareowners some economic freedom. They will have to work less for money, just as the technology they have financed is leaving less work to be done by human hands and minds.

WORK

Direct marketing of shareownership is part of the way we will resolve two issues that are behind many of our current difficulties: (1) How can we be happier in our work? and (2) How can we fairly share the wealth? This is not to say that entrepreneurs will go public, or individuals will buy shares in order to solve the world's problems. What it does mean is a more receptive market for shares, because people sense there is a way for them to become happier in their work and a way for them to share in business profits.

Some prospective investors will understand an entrepreneurial corporation's potential for fast growth and large profits. They can see the chance to make enough money so that they are less dependent on a paycheck. Other prospects, such as employees, subcontractors, suppliers, may envision how buying shares could help change the content of their own work, as new capital is invested in production technology. We are developing some different attitudes toward work, views that fit nicely with shareownership.

Work Can Make Us Feel Good

Our American work ethic came out of sixteenth-century Europe and the concepts of sin and redemption. From the English Statute of Artificers in 1563 to the U. S. Full Employment Act of 1948, it was accepted that everyone should work. We worked because that was our lot in life. Then we worked to consume. Reward in the afterlife was replaced with spending our way into heaven on earth. Work was still a means to an end, a necessary evil. Now we are learning that each of us can find a livelihood that will bring us a sense of purpose, peace and self-esteem. This belief that work can bring personal happiness fits with the new optimism that we can collectively find ways to improve life on our planet.

There is a growing acceptance that the world will not soon end from war or pollution or the exhaustion of its resources. People can, through their work and capital, develop ways to survive and to improve the quality of life.

If our objective is to get away from working just for money, then we need to create other money sources. Saving and earning interest is too slow. Gambling gives such poor odds. Investing in shares holds out the possibility that we can eventually work to feel good about ourselves and not just work for money.

Wealth Can Be Fairly Shares

It is not exactly that the rich get richer and the poor get poorer. From World War II until 1965, people at all income levels had big increases, on average. But the relative allocation remained about the same. The top fifth of American households got about 40% of the income and the bottom fifth got about 5%.

In the past ten years, the incomes of households in the bottom 40% have gone down, after inflation effect. Those in the top 20% continued to increase, most rapidly in the highest 5%.

Ownership of wealth is now much more concentrated. The Federal Reserve Board survey of 1983 consumer finances found that the 2% of households with incomes of more than $100,000 a year owned 28% of total household net worth, including 50% of corporate shares. The top 10% of households, by income, owned 57% of the net worth. Regarding this disparity, there is the often-quoted statement by Justice Louis D. Brandeis that "We can have democracy in this country or we can have great wealth concentrated in the hands of a few, but we can't have both." Discontent with this distribution comes in cycles. It will one day lead to a different allocation of wealth. The least disruptive way will be by helping workers become shareowners through direct marketing.

CHAPTER 3

Is Public Ownership Right for You?

Going public with your corporation can rank right up there with such major decisions as choosing your career or where you live. You go through the same process—imagining what it might be like, listing the pros and the cons.

HOW TO DECIDE WHETHER TO GO PUBLIC

There are a lot of big questions. You can reconsider and fine tune the answers as you move toward the offering process. For now, here is a modeling exercise to see if you should really be on the path toward an initial public offering.

Among the pros are the following:

Acceptance. This is the way that nearly every business goes, if it is to become significant.

Security. Having a large number of strangers owning shares means freedom from having a few lenders or investors looking over my shoulder.

Wealth. My best chance to build a really major estate, and to diversify my investments, is to go public.

Renown. To become well known for what I do, it is important to build a public company.

Altruism. Going public will benefit my employees and others who believe in the business.

Some of these may not be of interest or concern to you. But you will need some strong motivations to overcome the natural forces of inertia and such cons as:

Denial. There are other ways to finance and direct my corporation. I don't need public shareownership.

Insecurity. I may not be ready to have public shareowners relying on my ideas and abilities.

Fear. What if my corporation is rejected by investors, or my shareowners sue me?

Procrastination. I can stay private for now and reconsider later.

Laziness. It involves too much hassle with the SEC and snoopy shareholders.

There are some important questions vis-à-vis consideration of whether you and your corporation are right for public shareownership: Does public ownership fit your corporation? Are you ready to share the ownership of your corporation? Will your corporation appeal to individual investors? Are you clear about the amount you need? Do you have a clear idea of your purpose, and timing? See Table 3.1 for further clarification of these issues.

Table 3.1. What You Need to Know to Go Public

Does Public Shareownership Fit Your Corporation?
1. Is your corporation independent of ties to other corporations or family businesses?
2. Can you have public shareownership without imposing serious limitations on the corporate business?
3. Could the opportunities and problems of your business be explained openly and understandably to your target investors?

Table 3.1. (*continued*)

4. Do your auditors and lawyers go along with the concept of public shareownership?
5. Will public shareownership leave you free to comply with agencies that regulate your business?

Are you ready to share ownership of your corporation?
1. Are you able to separate the corporation from your personal image and identity?
2. Can you live with the possibility that you might one day be forced out of your job?
3. Will you be able to keep from paying your personal expenses out of the corporation?
4. Are you willing to have your compensation set by independent directors and disclosed in public documents?
5. Can you put up with a board of directors that may outvote you?

Will your corporation appeal to individual investors?
1. Can you explain the essence of the corporation in just a few words?
2. Would an investor have a good chance of seeing the share value double or triple within three years?
3. Are there people you know right now who could be counted on to buy at least 25% of the offering?
4. Can you identify groups of several thousand people who should have the interest and money to own your shares?
5. Are you willing to price your shares at a discount to their estimated market value?

Are you clear about the amount you need?
1. How much money would you be going for?
2. How much of your ownership would you be giving up?
3. What do you propose to do with the proceeds from the offering?

Do you have a clear idea of your purpose and timing?
1. Is your corporation in the right stage of its development to be going public?
2. Can you describe your plan for the business, going five years into the future?
3. Do you know when you expect to need more capital and how you would raise it?

AMOUNT OF THE OFFERING
AND PERCENTAGE OWNERSHIP

There is a lot of art in the pricing of a corporation, most especially in its initial public offering. Final decisions will be made after you have your whole offering team on board and up to speed. But you will need a pretty clear idea in mind when you decide to go public.

Going public involves a tradeoff between the amount of money raised and the percentage of the corporation you give up to public shareowners. Is $10 million for 25% fair? Is 40% really only worth $2.5 million, too small to make a public offering worthwhile? Take a look at a few corporations that are a lot like yours, except that they already have publicly traded stock. Figure some ratios of their earnings, revenues, and book value (assets minus liabilities) to their stock trading price. Talk it over with your accountant and other confidential advisers.

If your corporation has not yet received any significant revenues from its main business, you should probably continue looking to private money sources.

Sometimes, as with the birth of the biotechnology industry, public shareownership works to finance long start-ups. In most cases, the shares will usually not sell or, if they do, the new shareowners will become discouraged. The danger is then that you have ruined the corporation's image as a public company and have closed off that source of capital.

All you want at this point is some ballpark answer to (1) How much could you raise by giving up a comfortable percentage ownership—no more than 40%, and (2) does that amount make a public offering worthwhile—it needs to be at least $2 million and, more comfortably, more than $4 million?

You can estimate that fixed costs, such as legal, printing, and accounting fees, will run between $100,000 and $200,000. Marketing costs are harder to estimate, but the minimum to do the job is likely to be approximately 10% of the total offering price. Then you need to consider the strain on you and your staff. That often translates to lower earnings and lost opportunities for the business. Considering the fixed costs, the minimum needed for marketing, and the attention needed from management, it is hard to justify a public offering for less than $4 million.

Going for too little money is dangerous. Fixed costs will use too much of the proceeds. When the need arises again, the timing may be bad for another offering, either because of the general economy or because of a temporary setback in the corporation's results. Less obvious is the problem of having too large an initial public offering. If you raise more capital than you need, you will have given up more ownership of your corporation than necessary. As the corporate business advances through each stage of its development, you should be able to raise more and more capital by selling a smaller and smaller percentage shareownership.

A large, hidden cost of an initial public offering is a "new issue discount" that lowers the price by 20% or so, just because the shares have no trading history and the corporation is unknown. You only go through that discount once, so it helps not to sell more than you need to in the first round. As your corporation prospers and grows, the public will pay a higher price for each percent of ownership. You give up less per dollar in every successive round. After the first time, the other shareowners participate in that dilution of ownership. Each additional offering of new shares reduces the percentage ownership of the existing public shareowners, as well as your percentage. See Table 3.2 for an example of an offering program.

The kind of program shown in Table 3.2 will only work if you accept that marketing shareownership is a major part

Table 3.2. An Example of an Offering Program

Amount of the Offering	Percent of Ownership Sold	Founder's Ownership	
		Percent	Market Value
$5 million	25%	75%	$15 million
$10 million	20%	60%	$30 million
$10 million	10%	54%	$54 million
$25 million	10%	49%	$122 million

of your ongoing business. You cannot wait around for the experts to tell you that the market is right. Marketing share-ownership becomes a priority at the level of new product development, growth in market share, and cost control. It is your competitive edge, through access to low-cost, permanent capital. If you are ready to put selling shares at this level of corporate priority, then public shareownership can be right for you.

YOUR PURPOSE FOR BRINGING IN PUBLIC SHAREOWNERS

Whenever we are offered possessions the sellers have used for themselves, we naturally want to know why they are selling. Is this car about to break down? Have home prices hit their peak around here? The same thought process occurs when you are suddenly willing to sell a part of your corporation. Of course, it seems a lot less suspicious when you are keeping most of it for yourself. But you still need to express a clear answer to the question, "Why are you selling shares now?"

Your chance to tell that story will come by means of the prospectus—the legal document by which shares are sold. In the prospectus, one of the required sections is captioned "Use of Proceeds." This section tells the prospective investor what the corporation intends to do with the money received from selling shares. That can be woven into a description of the business plan—made a part of the story told by the prospectus.

Raising capital is not the only motivation for most initial public offerings. You may want to have publicly traded shares in order to set up an ESOP. Some of your private investors, who helped you get the business started, may need a way to get some cash from their holdings. Your bank may want to see some more equity capital as a cushion before it extends more credit. Customers may be more comfortable doing business with a public company, one they can expect to be around for a while.

Having a market may be part of your strategy for acquiring other businesses by issuing shares to their owners. All that makes sense and can help in marketing shares. What will not work as a purpose for the offering is a motive that takes away the investor's hopes and dreams. For instance, there are corporations that reach their optimum size rather quickly, perhaps corporations in retail or service businesses. The owner is satisfied with the operation, except for paying the interest on bank borrowings to finance inventory and receivables. Since dividends are not required on shares of common stock, how about replacing borrowings with shareowner money? It is clear what is in it for the owner, who can take out salary and benefits while plowing profits back into the business. But who wants to be an outside investor in a scheme for the sole benefit of the present owner? There has to be a basic element of "we're all in this together and we're shooting for the moon."

When Public Shareownership Does Not Fit

There are corporations that should not even be considered for public shareownership. Some corporations have a single, brief purpose. They may be organized around a business that is only temporary. Others may exist on the life cycle of a single product. A few corporations are merely convenient forms for individuals to sell their personal services. Doctors and lawyers are not yet permitted to share ownership of their professional businesses. Most entertainers and athletes have not chosen to sell shares in their careers. But advertising agencies and stock brokers have had public shareownership for years. It comes down to whether shares will sell and whether the corporate business can be operated fairly for both the shareowners and the corporation.

There are corporations in businesses that could not stand the publicity that would have to follow a public share offering. Others may be in regulated businesses that do not lend themselves to absentee ownership. Sometimes the corporation and its business may be good for the founders, but still not be a fair proposition for public shareowners. The basic investment proposition must (1) make sense and (2) convey real hope for shareowners to achieve their own personal goals through the investment.

Good Businesses May Be Bad Investments

A strategy can make good sense and have big potential for corporate insiders, yet be a "bum deal" for outsiders who buy at the public offering. Just as one example, the following discussion is a plan that is attractive to the founding group, but does not make sense for its new public shareowners.

The corporation is formed to go into a business arena filled with hundreds of small competitors, just as that business is being entered by some big players. By growing quickly through a public share offering, the corporation can get to a size where a big corporation will buy it out to increase market share.

If the plan is successful (a big if, based on the history of industry shakeouts in such arenas), the corporation is sold at a price that reflects the cost of getting rid of a competitor and buying some lead time. For the founders, that may be several times what they paid to get the corporation started. The public shareowners, who took a big risk on a long shot, are lucky if they break even. The founders can rest on their nest egg, with the prestige of having run a public company and sold out to a big corporation. The plan was a good one for them, but even the best scenario was a bad one for the investors.

Propositions that do not fit for public shareowners may do very well with other money sources. An example would be the grow-fast-and-sell-out strategy just described. That investment proposition could be just right for a debt financing, particularly if repayment were secured by corporate assets and personal guarantees from the founders. The lender might take some extra risk in return for rights to share in the gain from selling out

Innovation Overload

The fact is that shareownership is a new concept for the majority of us. It will take some time getting used to it. Meanwhile, we are most likely to get our feet wet as shareowners if there is a lot of comfort with the corporation—something simple and close to home. Innovation overload makes us feel confused and even claustrophobic. Too many new things at one sitting. That is when we are not likely to overcome our inertia and part with our money. If your corporation is at some cutting edge of technology or merchandising, perhaps it is better to wait awhile before seeking public shareownership. Combining new ideas in business with new ideas in shareownership may just be too much.

This advice could also be completely wrong for you. Your intuition or market research (or, better yet, both) may tell you that your future shareowners would love a chance to be way out there in effecting change. Just be aware.

Another early warning signal can be some regulatory obstacle that may limit or close off public shareownership. One obstacle that comes up frequently is the need for audited financial statements. If you have changed auditors recently, or if you have missed some major auditing standard, such as year-end inventory observations, it may be impossible to go public when you would like. If the obstacle is an auditing glitch, get a second and third opinion. There is ethical imagination to be found among accountants, although it sometimes takes some looking.

PUBLIC SHAREOWNERS AND THE LONE WOLF ENTREPRENEUR

Readiness for public shareownership begins with the values and attitudes of the entrepreneur. It takes a particular mix of personality traits to go from sole ownership to sharing "your" corporation with a thousand strangers, who expect you to take care of their investment as you do your own. Some entrepreneurs know they want a public corporation from the very beginning. Others accept it as the only way to pay for their plans. It can be an intuitive feel that sharing ownership is right. Or it can come from quantifying all the pros and cons.

Then there are entrepreneurs who would rather live with the limitations of private ownership than involve outside investors. That is clearly their right to choose. Individuals who would really like to participate as investors in that business are going to have to find a competitor—or help start one.

Some entrepreneurs may kid themselves into thinking they can operate with public shareownership, but, in fact, they may be unable to separate their corporation from their own personality. There are egos that extend into the corporate business and that could no more believe in sharing ownership of the corporation than they could accept giving up their arms or legs. Others who start businesses may prefer to share ownership with a few "partners," rather than with hundreds or thousands of strangers.

However the decision is reached, it is a very personal one. While a corporation is still owned by its founders, it is often an extension of their needs and desires. Later, the corporation will take on a character and value system of its own, derived from its shareowners, managers, workers, community, and customers.

Many corporations remain private because the entrepreneur is personally not suited to sharing ownership. A few of these have been willing to go against their nature and have a public offering anyway. This choice may work if the entrepreneur accepts that it is time for a change in role. For instance, the inventor/founder may turn over management to others, while finding satisfaction running a research laboratory. Financial security will have come from owning publicly traded shares and from signing an employment contract. Some entrepreneurs welcome exchanging the power and prestige of being boss for the freedom from pressures and anxieties that go with it.

One colorful entrepreneur had the lifetime goal of being the sole shareholder of a company listed on the NYSE. Since broad public shareownership is a requirement for listing, this was obviously impossible. But many entrepreneurs never reconcile themselves to the clear conflict between sharing ownership with outsiders and running the corporation as if it were their own household. Entrepreneurs need to be honest with themselves before they embark on the voyage of public ownership. And careful investors will detect the clues to future conflicts between an autocratic "owner" and the investors who are supposed to share that ownership.

A Steward for Shareowners

Commitment to public shareownership is the first issue. Competence for that step is the second. It is hard enough to run a small private business. You have to deal with taxes and licenses, bookkeepers and creditors, employees and customers. Then there are all the minor crises that could never have been anticipated. Public shareownership always adds new dimensions to these complications. An entrepreneur needs to achieve a sense of comfort and control over the elements of a private business before moving on.

Having a public company means much more than just the same issues in larger sizes. There is the nature of stewardship—taking care of someone else's interests. Every challenge is no longer "what's best for me" but becomes "what's best for the corporation and its shareowners." It is a different mindset, one that is alien territory to some of us.

Beyond honesty, public ownership means public disclosure. Candor takes on a new meaning in corporate stewardship. It becomes more than complying with the laws and meeting a personal code. There are disclosure obligations beyond those that might come naturally. One of the reasons some corporations stay private is to avoid the "fishbowl effect," through which actions are looked at by shareholders, analysts, regulators, and lawyers. Corporate managers need to be sensitive to what will look right, as well as what feels right and is within the law.

Imagining What Public Shareownership Would Be Like

Securities lawyers and investor relations consultants can give you an understanding of the impact of public shareownership. Another sensible step is to talk with fellow entrepreneurs who have gone through the transition to public shareownership. Imagine being in their shoes for a month or so.

Imagining through the experience of others is probably the best preparation for testing your own commitment and competence for public shareownership. Some entrepreneurs can get on the board of directors of a public corporation. Others may belong to an association that includes public corporations and fosters assistance at an open, intimate level. Sometimes the entrepreneur can spend a few days tagging along with a counterpart in a public corporation. Other windows on public shareownership include continuing education programs sponsored by organizations for lawyers, accountants, and executives, attending trade shows and talking with officers of public companies, and reading copies of company filings with the SEC.

The Right Time to Go Public

The decision about timing can mirror the decision on the amount of an offering. It becomes a major part of your corporate business plan and your personal objectives. Perhaps it is too soon. When corporate life begins, it is all dreams. Strangers may be excited by your dreams, but not many will pay to share them. Startups are for friends, relatives, and every dollar of your own.

When a beginning has been made, but there is not a steady growth of revenues, it will probably still be too soon for public shareownership. Some of the problems with going public while still in this bumpy, toddler stage are the following:

You will have to spend too much time and money educating your market about what you expect.

The percentage ownership you will have to offer may be too much for the cash you get in return.

Surprises happen more often and bigger early on, and they can frighten shareowners away.

Servicing costs of shareowner and SEC reporting are high for a single small sale.

This "sprout" stage, after operations have begun but before the proof of profits, is what venture capital is all about. But you have probably heard stories about what you may give up in order to get money from venture capitalists. Two choices you may lose are choosing when you will go public and deciding how you will market the shares. There can be less costly alternatives for getting through this development stage. For instance, your suppliers, key employees, and affluent acquaintances may be willing to invest privately if they see you have a practical plan for going public within two or three years.

Holding on Until the Time Is Right

Controlling costs during development, doing everything "on the cheap," is one way entrepreneurs have stayed out of the clutches of venture capitalists. Taking more time with development is often better than giving up the kind of control that venture capitalists have been demanding. This stage may seem so promising that you are now willing to tap some resources you left alone during the startup phase, such as your own borrowing power, loans from family or friends who would be using their "rainy day" funds, and from suppliers, customers, and employees. A caution on tapping friends, relatives, and business associates: When the time comes for the public offering, you may need some big hitters—individuals who buy in quantity and who are trendsetters for others. If they have been allowed in earlier, for a lot less money, you have lost this leverage.

Financing techniques are available to you in development that can help you keep control and have 100% ownership going into a first public offering. Creditors can be given rights to buy shares after the public offering. Customers can get incentives to pay in advance.

Your lawyer will caution you about having a string of negotiated stock sales that may be aggregated into a single, and illegal, public offering. Part of keeping it simple is avoiding any embarrassing delays when you file your public offering with the SEC and state securities administrators.

"Keep it simple" is a guiding principle in development stage financing. Legal, accounting, and marketing advice comes before any arrangements. Otherwise, you can find yourself trying to renegotiate terms with an investor at a time when you are over the barrel to make a public offering deadline.

Even when it is clear that your corporation will be accepted by public shareowners, timing issues still come up. Some of the dilemmas are that

1. You really need the money to move ahead now, but you'll be so much more profitable if you can get through next year. You'll have to sell 30% now, while next year you could get twice the money and sell only 20%.

2. This is when the corporate story would be most clear and promising to the investor markets you have in mind. But your plan calls for some steps next year that will hurt profits. How can you price an offering fairly now and not have the market price collapse on us later?

3. Borrowed money could get you through another 18 months, when the price to public shareowners could be a lot higher. But the balance sheet will look pretty risky, and you'll have to accept a lot of conditions from the lenders.

There are no easy answers to these kinds of questions. You have to make decisions in the way you have found works for you. A difference is that you can begin to appreciate the conflict between what is best for you, personally, and what is best for all the shareowners.

Corporations Without Investor Appeal

Corporations may be ready, and entrepreneurs may be willing, but some shares will probably just not sell. Marketing corporate shares means deciding who might like to invest in them and then communicating effectively with those people. Some businesses are not going to appeal to a sufficiently broad audience.

Your corporate business may be clear to you and yet look confusing to an outsider. It is usually easier to market a single concept than a multiline business. For example, making bicycle frames from a patented process suggests some target markets and a persuasive story. Adding the manufacture and lease of metal scaffolding, or the importing of bicycle parts, makes the market less clear and the story less focused.

It helps if your corporation has an uncluttered financial statement. Complex accounting strategies often reduce your taxes or accommodate some short-term financing, but they can mess up your balance sheet. Lengthy explanations are too much for most public offering prospects. Investors will also want to see where you plan to take the corporation and who is on board to get it there. Your basic business plan needs to come across in a few short sentences, and be met with a nod of the head and a muttered, "Ahh, that makes sense."

What Makes an Attractive Investment Proposition? Investors in young businesses sometimes say that the three most important things to look for are "management, management, and management." But most individual investors want more than good credentials and an honest face. We would rephrase the three most important standards as something like: "concept, management, and staying power."

Individuals who buy shares are deciding not to save that money for a future need, and not to spend it on a pleasure of the moment. We are expecting to give up the use of that money, for at least a year or so and maybe, if we decide to hang on to the stock, forever. In return, we must be offered a chance to realize a dream. There are insured deposits and government securities, whereby we can get our money back with interest and not take any risk. Or we can buy lottery tickets, for fun and the fantasy of being rich in a week. Sharing ownership of a young corporation is somewhere in between, and we need a way to evaluate the element of risk involved. Your basic investment proposition will need to (1) make sense and (2) convey real hope that investors could achieve some personal goals through share-ownership in your business venture.

The corporate concept needs to match some investor fantasies, but as an "investment." Shareownership has elements of both gambling and saving, so it has to generate the thrill of risk and, at the same time, sustain a rational analysis of that risk. Dreams of hitting it big have to be coupled with the comfort of not being taken for a fool. In this spectrum between gambling and saving, it is the concept behind the corporation that will attract most individuals. Perhaps some "pop star" of the corporate wars can say, "trust me to do something big," but most of us will want to make our own judgment on whether this is a successful plan.

Corporate Concepts. Learning whether you have an attractive business concept begins with the question: "attractive to whom?" Marketing your shares will require finding the natural constituencies for shareownership and persuading them to come aboard. At the beginning, it is only necessary to project whether the corporation is based on a concept that should have appeal to one or more groups, and whether those groups are likely investors in corporate shares.

Elements of the marketable corporate concept are that (1) it is exciting to people who share your interest in the subject, (2) the group of fellow enthusiasts represents enough money to buy your share offering, and (3) the story can be told simply, with documented facts and projections.

People Who Can Make It Happen.   You have the elements for a marketable corporate concept. Your corporation looks clean. It has an exciting yet reasonable story. Now you need a picture of management that looks capable of meeting the challenge. Individuals who are invited to be shareowners will ask whether your concept can be carried out by the people in charge. How this is answered becomes part of the share marketing program. But clever marketing is no substitute for the entrepreneur's informed conviction that the right team will be on the job. People who actually read prospectuses and annual reports often say they go from the first couple of pages back to the section on management, to see who is on the board of directors. If they are not impressed, they won't bother reading anything more.

Investors want to know that someone competent will be keeping the books and seeing that there is enough cash to pay bills on time. They need to feel there is a single boss who can manage this kind and size of business.

Your Role in the Corporation.   Inventors or other creative leaders are often not the right people to manage a corporation after it brings in public shareowners. Far better to face this issue before you go public than after. It is no good having the founder leave the helm after the offering. Better to move from president to chairman of the board ahead of time, while continuing to work full time on development and promotion. This is the very stuff of your dreams. No rule says you have to do everything, wear every hat. You have reached the stage where you can finally do what you like and what you do well. Before you begin the going-public process is the time to resolve any "is this all there is?" issues and settle into your role.

The Power to See It Through.   Staying power, the third essential, means adequate resources—in people, money, and access to supplies and markets. Before starting on the road to public shareownership, you and your management team will need to have imagined facing the worst-case scenario. A big one may be management succession. Who is there to step into your shoes—suddenly, if that should become necessary?

Also, the business plan will have to be based on some assumptions about sales, production, financing, and other events that are educated guesses. Staying power means the ability to keep the corporation going if those assumptions do not work out—assurance that the corporation can adjust, can hang in there, or do something to survive and move on with its program.

Measuring Your "Affinity Group Appeal"

First-time share offerings are not sold by the numbers, by comparative price-earnings or debt-to-equity ratios. There is too much risk involved to rely on estimates of future earnings and growth. Decisions are highly subjective. Most investors will have some personal interests that make them willing to take a chance on your shares. Identifying and measuring the buying power of these people is like the affinity group marketing used to sell such other financial products as insurance and credit cards. "Affinity groups" are segments of the public with interests that overlap with your business. Most obvious are employees, suppliers, distributors, and neighbors. Others are people whose work or play can make them believe in the value of your business.

Some corporations may be in businesses that seem dull and that barely earn enough to pay good salaries to their owner/managers. Without the hope of either fun or profit, strangers will have no attraction to shareownership. Other corporations may be in interesting, profitable businesses, but they will have trouble finding affinity groups with enough potential investors to make a successful share offering. The following is a list of factors which indicate that there are not likely to be affinity groups large enough to make a public offering possible.

1. There are only a handful of employees,
2. There are no brand names,
3. The corporation does no retail business,
4. The corporation handles a diffuse or intricate product,
5. The corporation deals with only a few suppliers,
6. The corporation is largely unknown in its local community, and
7. The corporation has no "celebrity" managers or directors.

There are techniques to quantify whether your corporate shares will sell, and at a price you can live with. The following outline can aid you in doing so.

1. From your experience, and talking with others, describe the markets you think exist for the shares.
2. Put those markets into groups, based on the average amount each investor would likely invest.
3. Estimate the number of individuals in each group you would be trying to reach with your marketing program.
4. Apply your best-informed guess as to the percentage of each group that would buy shares.
5. Multiply the numbers in 2, 3 and 4, and add the resulting amounts.

Table 3.3. Model for a $10 Million Offering of Shares

Average Investment	Number in Group	Percentage Who Would Buy	Amount for the Group
$100,000	100	30%	$3,000,000
$ 40,000	2,000	3%	$2,400,000
$ 10,000	12,000	2%	$2,400,000
$ 2,500	100,000	1%	$2,500,000
	Total Investment		$10,300,000

If you figure you could probably be successful with a $10 million sale of shares, the formula would look like the one in Table 3.3.

As you get into this kind of marketing analysis, you are ready to consider how you will choose to market your shares. Should you use a securities firm to do an underwritten offering? Is that option available to you? What about marketing your shares directly to investors, without an underwriter?

CHAPTER 4

How an Underwritten
IPO Is Done

The basic concept of an underwritten IPO is that part of a corporation is sold to an underwriter, who then resells it, in much smaller pieces. A managing underwriter usually divides the sale among other securities firms in an underwriting syndicate.

THE MECHANICS OF
AN UNDERWRITTEN IPO

The corporation's steps are to find an underwriter, negotiate the terms, and go through the preparation process. It is then up to the managing underwriter to put together the syndicate and see that its members do their job.

Shopping for a Managing Underwriter

This step may be over before it begins. If there is to be an underwritten IPO, the choice of managing underwriter is often predetermined. An entrepreneur may already be tied in with a securities firm that manages IPOs, one with the required capacity and commitment. This often happens when venture capital financing has been arranged through a securities firm or its affiliate.

IPO underwriting is not really price competitive. Commissions are 8 to 10%. Underwriters also get warrants to buy additional shares during the first five years, at a price pegged to the underwriting. Any difference in terms between underwriting firms becomes insignificant compared to the larger issues of pricing the shares, timing the sale, and the firm's reputation for completing underwritings. Whether an underwriter can be made interested depends on timing. There are cycles in underwritten IPOs, times when nearly any entrepreneur can go public and times when the entire new-issues market seems shut down. The number of underwritten IPOs has peaked at more than 1,000 one year, 1969, only to go below 30 in 1975. Within the cycles are the fads. If a company is part of the favored industry, investment bankers will seek it out and rush its shares to market. A year or two earlier or later, no one will touch it. Entrepreneurs who plan to go public will monitor market activity to sense when a new-issues boom is developing and when interest is turning to their industry. They subscribe to magazines and newsletters that follow the new-issues market. These entrepreneurs develop information channels to securities analysts and watch their industry peers.

When the time looks favorable, an entrepreneur checks to see which securities firms have been managing IPOs for similar corporations. Meetings with as many as a dozen firms are set—through friends, a securities lawyer, or directly. Preparation for the meeting is mostly in gaining an understanding of how investment bankers react and make decisions. Publications and speeches emphasize that the company should have a thoroughly documented business plan, at least a million dollars in profit, $10 million in sales, and a 20% growth rate. Experience shows that what really works is being in the right business and making the right impression on investment bankers

One securities lawyer/underwriting advisor, Dennis O'Connor, told the Chief Executive Officers Club in Los Angeles, on July 8, 1988:

> The ability of a company to go public is primarily a function of market climate, not the operational performance of that particular company. The next thing that is most important is the manner of selecting and presenting your situation to an underwriter, or group of underwriters. And only lastly is the operational performance critical.

Shopping for an underwriter becomes a matter of selling the entrepreneur and the corporate image, then selecting among the firms that show an interest. Then it is time for a letter of intent.

The Letter of Intent

When the entrepreneur and securities firm have chosen each other, the underwriter furnishes a letter of intent. It says that the underwriter will buy shares to be issued, as soon as the offering is cleared with the SEC and state securities regulators. A price range and number of shares are set.

Those who have not been through an underwriting usually believe that a handshake and letter equal a firm commitment, that the underwriter has agreed to buy the shares, and assume the risk of reselling them. But the letter of intent is just what its name implies. There is nothing at all about it that is legally enforceable, except the corporation's obligation to pay the underwriter's expenses if the entrepreneur calls off the sale. An obligation to buy the shares does not exist until the underwriting agreement is signed. That happens only after the shares have been resold. There is no commitment to buy until the selling is done.

For purposes of signing an underwriting agreement, the selling is done when stockbrokers have gathered "indications of interest" from their customers. Legally, there can be no sale until the customer has received a final prospectus that has been processed through the SEC. The prospectus is sent along with a confirmation of the sale and the customer has five days to pay for the shares or to back out, to renege. Underwriters try to have indications of interest for 150% of the total number of shares, to cover reneges. The underwriting risk, that of being left holding unsold shares, is limited to the few days in which customers may renege. Most underwriters will also take on some risk in buying and selling shares after the offering, to stabilize the market price.

A letter of intent is about three pages long and covers only a few topics. Among those may be lock-up or "green shoe" issues.

Lock-up. Most people buy underwritten new issues in the hope that they can soon resell the shares at a higher price, because demand will have exceeded the supply in public hands. This image requires that the shares held by the founders be kept off the market until the underwriter's customers have had a chance to take their profit. So the private shareowners are expected to "lock up" their shares for three months to a year after the IPO.

Green Shoe. Underwriters may find that fewer buyers renege then expected, so they have to deliver more shares than they have agreed to buy. To cover the shortage, underwriters buy shares in the trading market. This can drive the price above the offering and create losses to the underwriting syndicate. In an IPO by the Green Shoe Manufacturing Company (now the Stride Rite Corporation), underwriters first obtained an option to buy more new shares, at the same underwriting price, "to cover overallotments." To keep the option from being open-ended, the National Association of Securities Dealers put a limit on the Green Shoe equal to 10% of the number of shares being underwritten. In 1983, this limit was raised to 15% of the underwriting.

Other provisions may give the underwriter the right to do future financings, arrange a buyout by another company, and appoint a representative to the board of directors.

This is the structure for a "firm commitment" underwriting. A securities firm can also agree to use its "best efforts" to sell shares, usually with a minimum and maximum number. Very few best-efforts IPOs are done, and each one is tailormade, unlike the rigid formula for a firm commitment IPO. Firms that do best-efforts offerings are not the ones invited into underwriting syndicates. Entrepreneurs are told that it is a second-rate way to go public and could ruin the corporation's reputation in the capital markets.

The Preparation Process

Management of the IPO preparation process usually falls to the lawyers, either those for the corporation or for the underwriter, depending on experience and personality. The first thing the lawyers do is schedule an "all-hands" meeting, inviting corporate officers, investment bankers, auditors, financial printers, and anyone else who will be important in the proceedings.

There will be four to six of these all-hands meetings over the four months or so of preparation. They usually last 8 to 16 hours a day for 1 to 3 days. The first meeting is held to go over a schedule of the steps involved, figure out who is responsible for each step, and what the deadlines are. Major issues may come up, such as legal and accounting barriers to a public offering, or whether the corporate name should be changed. More sensitive subjects, like changes in the board of directors, are discussed at a private dinner between the entrepreneur and the investment bankers.

One of the teams of lawyers will prepare the first draft of the prospectus, the document that is sent to investors with the confirmation of their order for shares. The remaining all-hands meetings are mostly prospectus-editing sessions. All-hands meetings are also part of the "due dili-gence" process. Underwriters and others involved in the IPO can be liable to investors for misrepresentations and omis-sions in the prospectus. Securities laws provide a defense for those underwriters and other IPO-involved people who use due diligence in reviewing the corporate history and other facts that should be important to investors.

There will be a "night at the printer's" just before the prospectus is filed with the SEC and state "blue sky" (state securities) regulators. This last-minute editing ritual will be repeated when any amendments are filed in response to comments from SEC reviewers.

Tension really begins to build when the amended pro-spectus is filed. There are usually only three more weeks until the "effective date," when the prospectus is cleared and confirmations of sale can be mailed. The investment bankers will be calling the entrepreneur with the latest news from their syndicate department—what securities firms want to be included, how many shares have been "circled" by a brokerage office and which mutual fund man-agers have shown an interest. There will be both good and bad news, always with uncertainty about whether the shares will get sold and what the final price will have to be. The climax comes the night before the effective date, when the entrepreneur and investment bankers agree on the price and sign the underwriting agreement.

Selling the Shares

During that last three weeks before the effective date, the managing underwriter's syndicate department begins put-ting together an underwriting syndicate of securities firms. Each member of the syndicate has an allotment of shares that it is responsible for buying under the "Agreement Among Underwriters." There is a "Selected Dealer Agree-ment," (see Glossary) for local securities firms that are not in the syndicate but are allowed to sell shares for a split of the commission.

The "red herring."   A final draft of the legal offering document, the preliminary prospectus, helps firms decide whether they want into the syndicate and how many shares they expect to sell. The bold red letters on the cover explain that the preliminary prospectus is only a red herring, used to build interest in the real thing to follow.

Underwriting commissions (the spread) are divided three ways: The managing underwriter keeps 20%; another 20% is for the underwriting syndicate, although it is used to pay for the underwriters' legal and other expenses; and the remaining 60% is for the firm whose broker gets the customer's order. The split between the firm and its broker will vary, but is usually about 60% for the firm and 40% for the broker.

Names gathered from the entrepreneur, directors, and employees are usually turned over to the managing underwriter's own brokers for processing the order. Investment bankers insist that all shares be sold in the underwriting. The managing underwriter prepares an internal memorandum, to help the syndicate candidates decide whether they can sell an allotment. This often becomes a four-page flyer for individual brokers to use in their telephone calls to customers and prospects. There is a summary of the business, capsule financial information, key selling points, and ways to answer questions investors might ask. Key phrases are in boldface type.

The Road Show.   In addition to telephone selling by syndicate brokers, there are due diligence meetings for institutional money managers, at which corporate officers answer questions and make an impression. This comes just before the underwriting agreement is to be signed and may include a week in Europe and Japan, as well as a week traveling across the United States.

Many brokers know which of their customers want to hear about new issues and who might be interested in a particular industry. By concentrating on these prequalified customers, they can reach a favorable ratio of shares sold to calls made. A "hot new issue" is an IPO that becomes effective at the peak of a fad for its industry. These provide brokers with a chance to reward customers and attract prospects by letting them have some of their allotted shares.

Competition among investment bankers is based on their ability to get transactions done. Word of failures gets around. Rivals see to that. To maintain a reputation, it may be necessary for an underwriter to go through with an offering when there are orders for less than all the shares. Although they have no legal obligation under the letter of intent, their competitive sense of prestige may lead them to risk owning leftover stock at a price above the aftermarket.

HOW UNDERWRITTEN IPOs CAME TO BE THAT WAY

The concept of corporate shareownership began when business ventures started needing more capital than the entrepreneur could provide. Sixteenth-century merchant ships became the model for corporate IPOs.

Corporations, Shares, and the Stock Exchange

Ships were expensive to build, and a crew and supplies had to be financed until the "ship came in." And someone had to bear the risk, for all could be lost at sea. Entrepreneurs began selling shares in the ships and voyages. Courts developed precedents for dealing with disputes that arose over the rights of shareowners. When railroads and big manufacturing enterprises came along, legislatures had created the corporation as a separate "person," able to enter contracts, to be defended by the courts and police, to enjoy nearly every right but voting. Rules were made to serve the economic realities. Most important was the concept that a shareowner is not at risk for anything except the amount paid for the shares: No fear of "my partner ruined me." No calls for more money. No contingent liabilities.

Stock exchanges were organized as places for people to get in and out of shareownership. This brought the magic of liquidity. The corporation could keep forever the money it got from selling shares. But shareowners could sell for cash at any time. With a stock trading market, an entrepreneur could offer investors shareownership in a way that let shareowners cash out at any time, limited their loss to the price they paid, and provided them with clear legal rights. In return, the entrepreneur got money that never had to be paid back, required no interest payments ever, and left management free to run the business.

As corporations increased in number and size, making a market for stocks grew into a business of its own. The customer base for the new securities industry was the growing class of investors—people who bought stock for the long haul, because they believed in the business concept and its management.

Brokers, Traders, and Dealers

The financial intermediary roles in the stock market came to be the following:

> **Brokers.** They perform the market mechanics and provide a source of information and advice,
>
> **Traders.** They create an active market through frequent speculative buying and selling, and
>
> **Dealers.** They make markets liquid through continuous buying and selling.

Brokers act as the agents for investors and traders, matching orders to buy and to sell. As the market grew, with more choices available, investors needed a source of information and expert opinion about companies and their stocks. Brokers were willing to fill this need, getting paid by commissions from executing the resulting buy-and-sell orders.

Traders make a business of buying and selling shares for a speculative, short-term profit. They help give the market a volume of activity that allows prices to be quoted on a regular basis.

Dealers are in the business of buying and selling for their own account, making small price markups as they turn over their inventory, and smoothing out price fluctuations. A dealer may be a specialist on an exchange or a market maker for shares traded over-the-counter, where their function is to balance the flow of buy-and-sell orders. Dealers may also buy large blocks of stock and redistribute them among many buyers.

Since the 1800s, these functions have served to keep a trading market for shares of corporate ownership going. Most of the Wall Street securities firms are brokers, traders, and dealers, all at once. They are also the underwriters of IPOs, but that is not the way it began.

Underwriters

Historically money to build and launch ships was raised by selling shares among the merchant class. As the Industrial Revolution began, English joint-stock companies were financed the same way.

Insuring the Risk of Unsold Shares. There was always the risk that enough shares would not have been sold by the time the money was needed. So the early entrepreneurs went to people in the business of "underwriting" risks. The original underwriters were insurance companies that would agree to purchase any shares left unsold in return for an underwriting fee. To spread the risk of large stock issues, the insurance companies joined together in underwriting syndicates. So the original underwritten IPOs were marketed directly by their entrepreneurs, who paid underwriters to assume the risk of an uncompleted offering.

Purchasing Shares for Resale. Corporate shares began to be used as a medium of exchange in commercial transactions. Money, in the sense of government currency, was not that reliable. Commercial banks and large merchants began purchasing new issues of corporate shares as a way of investing extra cash and settling accounts. This investing and trading led to buying new issues of stock from entrepreneurs, for resale. For the larger issues, the merchants and banks began forming syndicates to share the marketing, with an allotment of shares to each syndicate member. The risk of unsold shares was divided the same way. Eventually, firms began to specialize in financings.

Investment Bankers

By 1900, after the vast railroad financings, there were a dozen or so major firms that would market the shares of any public offering. They had become specialists in corporate finance and called themselves investment bankers. These few firms became respected and powerful. When investors and traders bought an IPO, it was based on the reputation of the investment banker. If an entrepreneur could not convince one of these titans to underwrite the new issue, it just did not happen. Owning corporate shares was still limited to the wealthy few, and they relied on the likes of J. P. Morgan's firm and a handful of others to screen the right companies. There had been too many stock market "panics" since the Civil War for them to take a chance on their own. Endorsement was what investment bankers had most to offer. Their contribution was not so much selling as it was placing their stamp of approval on a stock.

Investment Bankers Transformed. Before the 1920s, investment bankers dealt with a few wealthy families in Europe and the United States. Not many people trusted financial assets, values represented only by pieces of paper. Attitudes toward investing were changed by the immense success of Liberty Bonds sold by the U. S. Treasury to finance World War I. They were printed in small denominations and could be bought on the installment plan. Securities firms were used to sell the bonds into a market estimated in 1917 at only 350,000 individuals. In fact, the first series of bonds was subscribed by more than 4 million people and, by the fourth bond issue, there were more than 22 million investors.

According to Vincent P. Carosso in his book, *Investment Banking in America: A History*, (Cambridge: Harvard University Press, 1970), after the war was over:

> A vast new group of investors had been revealed throughout the land . . . . The public demand for securities, stimulated by advertising and promotional campaigns, was insatiable, and the profits to be made in underwriting and distributing new issues lucrative. The result was a marked decline in banking judgment and ethics and unscrupulous exploitation of public gullibility and avarice.

In Carosso's opinion, the Crash of 1929 and the congressional investigations that followed, "Completed the transformation of the investment banker's image from the folk hero of the prosperity years to the scapegoat of the Depression era." Congress passed laws, creating the SEC and making crimes of practices that had contributed to the Crash. One of the laws would have separated brokers and dealers, so one firm could not act as agent for customers and also be buying and selling securities for its own account. That would have taken underwriting away from brokerage firms. That provision was lobbied out at the last moment.

Another attack on investment bankers came in an antitrust case, *U.S. v. Morgan*, tried before Judge Harold Medina in the U. S. District Court for the Southern District of New York, whose opinion is reported in 118 F. Supplement 621 (1953). The Justice Department had charged 17 Wall Street firms with monopolistic practices in underwriting corporate securities. Judge Medina dismissed the case after the government's side was presented and it was never appealed.

UNDERWRITTEN IPOS TODAY

Underwritten IPOs have become an ever-tighter bottleneck for the flow of capital from individuals to entrepreneurs. Changes in the securities industry have been the major cause, as is described in detail in Chapter 1. Investment bankers are not preparing IPOs, and underwriting syndicates are not selling them. But the problem is not all in the diminished capacity to prepare and distribute IPOs. Entrepreneurs who can attract an underwriter still have many reasons to look for alternatives to an underwritten IPO. For instance, the way the shares are sold, who buys the shares, and how the process is managed all have inherent negatives.

How the Shares Are Sold

Telemarketing can be useful as one component of a marketing program. But all by itself, telephone selling is usually not an effective way to introduce a complicated new product. Yet it is the only marketing tool used in an underwriting, even though the prospect is someone who has probably never heard of the corporation being sold.

Brokers have only a minute or two to arouse some interest, and then another few minutes to close the sale. There is no market research to help package the offering and target likely investors. There is no strategy about what aspects of the business should appeal to what kind of person. There is no supporting message in print or electronic media. No one trains the brokers about the corporation.

Who Buys the Shares

In an underwritten offering, the corporation gives up any say over who buys the shares. These are the people with whom the entrepreneur is going to share ownership. Yet their identity is determined by the underwriter's priorities, not the corporation's. The new shareowners' first impression of the corporation will have come from a broker who probably first learned of the company a day or two before.

The entrepreneur will never know what was said to induce a purchase of the shares.

Underwritten IPOs are the last holdout from the days of fixed commissions. That means that a selling broker can make $5,000 from calling a money manager who buys 10,000 shares, as compared to making $50 from calling an individual who buys only 100 shares. Why bother with individuals if the whole issue can be sold to a relative handful of people who buy for institutions? And why do any underwritings at all unless they can be sold to institutional investors? This leaves the corporation with, maybe, 500 shareowner names after it has gone public. Since most of those will be institutions, there are probably only 100 decision makers involved. One money manager may put the shares into several different client accounts.

The underwriter is the common bond among all these investors, especially if the entire issue has been sold without a syndicate of other brokerage firms. That means they are all likely to react to future news in the same way at the same time, leading to price swings of as much as 50% or more in a day or two. This further discourages any individual investors and keeps ownership concentrated.

How the Process Is Managed

Underwritten IPOs generally lack any real process management. Lawyers usually take charge of the schedule, since so much depends on writing the prospectus and getting regulatory clearance. Accountants go off to do their job, and come back to argue with the lawyers. Financial printers are the servants of the lawyers and usually spare no expense to accommodate them.

An entrepreneur's only recourse to control the price, timing, and expense is to call the whole thing off. Otherwise, the corporation will go public when the underwriter says the market is favorable, the price will be what the underwriter says is necessary to get the deal done, and the corporation will pay the expenses that have mysteriously built up since the process began.

WHEN AN UNDERWRITTEN IPO
MAKES SENSE

Even with these problems, an underwritten IPO may still work for some corporations today. Those include situations in which the corporation is already in the hands of custodial management, when the objective is to cash out private investors, when going public is just a step in a strategy to sell out entirely, and when the entrepreneur is confident that one public offering is all that will ever be needed.

Accommodating Custodial Care

Control of a corporation sometimes passes to managers who have no ownership interest. The entrepreneur may have died or been ousted. Those in charge may be motivated by the first principles of bureaucracy: (1) avoid work, (2) have a clean record, and (3) network to a better job.

Work can be avoided by turning over the going-public project to an underwriter and the lawyers. Hiring a name securities firm shifts responsibility for the financing away from the manager's record. Getting to know corporate finance people in major securities firms, and granting favors to some of them, can be seen as the big chance to move on as a winner.

Cashing Out Investors

Venture capitalists and other private investors need an exit plan when they decide to invest. It is not enough to have the corporation be successful if there is no way for the financial backers to realize their profit. An entrepreneur can avoid being forced to sell the whole business if investors can be cashed out in a public market.

Some recent IPOs have really been extensions of venture capital financing. Buyers at the public offering have been a handful of institutional money managers. But the IPO will have generated some trading among big investors, providing a chance to unload all or part of an early private stake. Several IPO underwriters (e.g., Hambrecht & Quist, Alex Brown & Sons Inc. and Robertson, Stephens & Co.) have close relationships with venture capital firms and have an interest in helping them cash out.

A strategy of cashing out through an underwritten IPO is very much a timing game, often requiring years of waiting. There has not been a favorable climate for underwritten IPOs since the first half of 1983. For one company, Diasonics, a manufacturer of medical diagnostic imaging equipment, the payoff was immense. It raised $123 million in February 1983, at a price equal to 89 times its 1982 earnings. As reported in the February 24, 1983 *Wall Street Journal*, institutional investors were "jostling to get higher allotments of Diasonics stock." An unnamed institutional money manager was quoted as saying, "I wouldn't know a Diasonics if it hit me on the head. But I pay a lot of commissions to some of these brokers, and I got some shares." A reason cited by the *Journal* for the IPO's success "is its affiliation with some of the top names in venture capital and with securities firms that have brought out other high-technology offerings."

Preparing to Sell It All

Founding investors often start a corporation with the objective of selling out when they can reach a target price. Going public can accelerate that process. Investment bankers who do underwritings also look for follow-on fees from arranging acquisitions, and the letter of intent can specifically provide them with that opportunity. Being public brings a corporation to the attention of prospective buyers and provides readily accessible information.

Doing an IPO not only invites acquisition interest, it can increase the acquisition price. When a company is privately owned, negotiations for its acquisition involve pricing formulas related to earnings, sales, and assets. Public stock trading generally brings much higher valuations. Since management would never sell at less than the market price, going public can establish a floor on any future acquisition price.

Going Only Once to the Well

Most disadvantages of an underwritten IPO have to do with what happens after the sale—the trading market, future stock offerings, relations with shareowners. There may be entrepreneurs who are not concerned about those issues because they never expect to need shareowner money again. They may plan to wait for the price to drop and then buy the shares back. If the corporation's business coincides with a new-issues fad, it can make sense to say 'yes' when an investment banker suggests doing an IPO. The stock price may drop when the fad passes. Shareowners may become disillusioned. But if the entrepreneur is convinced that a one-time injection will last forever, doing an IPO may be worth it.

CHAPTER 5

How to Sell Shares Through Direct Marketing

Corporate shares can be sold with the same basic tools we use to market other consumer products. It has been done successfully. And it is legal. This chapter is a step-by-step program for an entrepreneur to sell shares through direct marketing. To begin with, you have a corporation with the commitment and competence to handle public shareowner-ship. It has the appeal of concept, management, and stay-ing power. But it is probably not ready to meet the public.

PREPARING YOUR CORPORATION
TO GO PUBLIC

Having a good investment proposition is just the beginning of the marketing process. Shareownership in your corpora-tion needs to be attractively and safely packaged. Then there will be the design, testing, and carrying out of a marketing program. Packaging your shares includes some corporate cleanup, image issues, selecting a board of directors, and making some decisions about the mechanics of how the corporation will be governed.

Corporate Cleanup

"Corporate cleanup" is a securities lawyer's term used to describe the rearranging and tidying up of the corporate affairs. Some of those are minor, such as proper minutes for meetings of directors and shareholders. Others can be touchy, such as getting rid of devices you may have used to save taxes, take care of family members, or protect the original investors. When you were the sole shareowner, decisions of corporate structure are likely to have been dictated by tax advisers, bankers, and by chance. The result may not lend itself to public shareownership.

Land and buildings, and related mortgages, may belong in or out of the corporation, depending on their importance to the corporate business. If they are not to be property of the corporation, this real estate should be owned by outsiders and under long-term leases. Clean, simple, predictable. Airplanes, mountain retreats, club memberships, and expensive cars are sometimes accumulated in private corporations, with some fuzziness between business and personal use. You could no doubt defend their value to the corporate purpose. Get rid of them. Shares are not sold by good defenses.

Some discoveries may delay the offering, like finding that shares sold to friends and associates along the way were technically an illegal "public offering." It is not unusual for the offering to be abandoned for a couple of years because audited financial statements cannot be produced to satisfy the securities laws.

Image Issues

Your corporation will be making a first impression. It will be giving signals about its true identity. You want to have that image be accurate and persuasive. Here are some of the issues:

Corporate Name. Your own ego and sentiments need to be balanced with what the corporate name communicates to prospective investors, how it will fit your vision of the future.

Headquarters. Your address will communicate whether you are a part of daily operations or in a remote control tower, whether you are a home town business or a financial center operation.

Corporate Structure. Holding companies and multiple subsidiaries may be necessary for your kind of business. Generally, the simpler the better.

The Business You Are In. Your concept has to be understood at first glance. This may be the time to create your concept's expression through a corporate slogan or a new logo. Going public has caused companies to hire a corporate image consultant.

Culture. In direct marketing, you are letting in another group of participants. They need to have some feel for the atmosphere. Is this a "one big happy family" organization or is it formal and serious?

Outside Professionals. You hire your law firm, auditors, and other professionals according to your own standards. Their names will communicate an image by association. If you are willing to consider a change, now is the time to do it.

Most important to your corporate image will be the people on your team—management and the board of directors. Image may not influence your choice of executives, but it is certainly appropriate in picking directors.

The Board of Directors

Corporations are structured like parliamentary governments—directors are elected by all the shareholders to make policy decisions and to appoint executives to carry them out. Before you go public, the board of directors is handpicked by you and your initial backers. Now you need to present a board that can represent the interests of your new public shareowners as well.

Selection of directors is among the most neglected of corporate decisions. Entrepreneurs are often casual about it, considering directors to be a technical necessity. Some become obsessed with personal loyalty and load the board with relatives and cronies. When most of us pick up a prospectus, we first get a general impression of the business and then we flip to the parts we feel competent to understand—the people. We make some quick judgments about the officers and directors. We will be more inclined to learn more, and buy your shares, if your selection of directors inspires confidence and comfort.

Such qualities as independence, competence, and commitment, are what investors are looking for.

Independence.   Are we really sharing ownership in this corporation, or are we just giving you our money, without any say in what happens? If the directors are your management team, relatives, and business associates, then we have to put all our faith in you alone. If you are the only insider on the board, then we can feel that there can be some balance if necessary.

Competence.   A director's competence can be related to the corporation's product or service—academic research in the technology, a professional in the end user market for the product, a retired executive from a related business. Competence can also come in the form of one of the major corporate processes—someone who was chief executive officer of a corporation throughout its public offering and successful growth, a whiz at marketing your kind of markets, a major investor who brings common sense to complex accounting issues.

Commitment.   This quality is best shown by shareownership. Particularly impressive is a statement that the director intends to buy a significant number of shares at the same time and price as the public. You may have let them own shares earlier, at a much lower price. It helps if they plan to buy more shares at the public offering. People understand that some directors can afford to invest more money than others, and that no one (but you) should be tying up too much in one corporation.

If the professor on the board invests $10,000 and the major investor puts in $100,000, that will probably look like commitment for both.

Picking a board of directors can even be a part of the share marketing campaign. Some entrepreneurs have been very blunt about establishing an "entry fee" to be on the board. They require that each director buy at least a certain amount of shares in the public offering. This needs to be disclosed to other prospective investors. Properly handled, it can be a positive quality.

Corporate Governance

This is one of those subjects that is periodically all the rage among politicians and academicians. Most people never think about it—until they suddenly feel slighted by the way an issue has been handled. Corporate governance means: "Who is in charge here and how do I get treated fairly?" Corporations are governed by their charters and bylaws, which describe how groups of interested people are to relate to each other. Most issues of corporate governance have to do with the relationship between shareowners and management. Before you take your corporation public, the shareowners and the management will probably be the same people. But you will need to make some choices now with an eye to possible future conflict.

You formed your corporation by filing papers with a state agency. If it is not the one in which you are headquartered, the selection probably was based on the rights of management, directors, and shareowners. You will have to explain some of those rights in the prospectus. Reincorporating from your home state to Delaware, for instance, may suggest that corporate governance is going to tilt in favor of management over shareholders.

Basic to corporate governance is whether you will have more than one class of shares. When some big private corporations finally went public, the founding family ended up with more votes per share than the class of stock sold to investors. Sometimes the dividend rights are different on the insider class than on the outsider class. If your corporation is already well known, there may possibly be plenty of demand for shares that are second class to the ones you keep. But in most cases, you will have only one class— common stock.

Cumulative voting becomes important with one class of stock. Without it, the owners of just over 50% can elect all the directors. Cumulative voting means that directors can be elected in proportion to shares owned. If there are seven directors, for instance, one of them could be elected by people owning only 15% of the shares.

You will decide whether the entire board is up for election each year or is a staggered board, in which a third of the directors are elected each year for three-year terms. Staggered boards can turn shareowner revolutions into evolutions. Then there are management protections like supermajority voting and "poison pills." In almost every corporation, it will be best to keep it simple, standard, and favorable to investors. Remember that you will be asked to explain anything that is not.

SELECTING THE TEAM

If you want to build your company with public capital, selling shares will become a continuous part of your corporate business. Daily activities will be influenced by their possible effect on shareholders. In the continous marketing of shareownership, everyone within the corporation is on the team. This sounds like a lot of work. It is. But you do not have to do it yourself. Look upon public shareownership as a profit center. The "income" is what you save in borrowing costs, the freedom from loan agreement restrictions, the ability to grow more rapidly than you could with money from banks or private investors. Viewed this way, you can afford to have a team devoted to servicing shareowner capital.

Your initial public offering is a special effort. It will have a beginning, end, and measurable stages. The process is like a political campaign: Lots of strategy planning, dealing with the unexpected, building to a peak—and then it is over until the next offering. This special effort calls for its own team. Some of the members of your public offering team will be independent contractors, on board for the duration of the project. Others will be employees, permanent and temporary, full time or part time.

Essential members of the team include your project manager, numbers person, securities lawyer, and advertising agency. Each of those roles is described here, as well as several others you are likely to need.

Project Manager

The captain of the team should be a full-time employee of the corporation, but *not* the chief executive or chief financial officer. It won't help to have you miss opportunities and ignore warning signs because a successful share offering became the obsession of your work life.

That kind of obsession is just what the project manager should have so that the share offering's success is not just top priority, but the only major concern for the six months or so it will be underway. If the manager is called off on another matter for even a few hours, the message to the rest of the team runs against all they have been told about the importance of their project. Nothing so promotes success as the singleminded dedication of the project manager.

When it comes to running the share offering, your project manager needs to have all the authority of the chief executive, and be specifically backed by the board of directors. When asking for information from employees not on the team, or talking with the corporate lawyers or accountants about the share offering, the project manager should receive the same treatment as you would expect for yourself.

When someone comes to you to complain or to test (and it will surely happen), your project manager will need your unwavering support, whatever private discussions you may later have.

One of the most successful share offering captains was a recently retired top legal officer for the corporation. It was a great advantage to have someone who knew everybody, but did not have to work with them after the offering was over.

Another corporation had a successful offering almost in spite of making a classic management mistake. The president, who expected to retire in a few years, had refused to designate his successor. Then he appointed as co-managers of the going public project the two executive vice presidents who were competing for his job. Their rivalry was played out in the scramble to take credit and avoid blame for each project decision. The experience did some lasting injury to the corporation.

Most young companies will not have someone they can spare for this six month period. You may be able to hire a project manager who can later move into a permanent position. There will be the risk of an unknown quantity, and you may have to be more personally involved than is ideal. But someone who comes through as a successful project manager will likely have a lot to contribute to the ongoing business. It may work for you to hire an independent contractor to be project manager. As a result of a series of recent direct share offerings, there are now experienced people who can sign on for the duration and report directly to the chief executive.

Numbers Person

Numbers become very important in explaining the corporation and in meeting securities law standards. Gathering financial information and presenting it effectively can chew up huge blocks of time. You need someone who is smart, understands accounting, works well under pressure, and gets along with people—those are the qualifications for the chief financial officer in your fast-growing business. If you do not yet have such a person in your management, you may want to fill the gap before you proceed with the offering.

Outside auditors are qualified to do this gathering and presenting. But paying their billing rates is just the beginning of the extra cost. Because they are auditors, they accept some professional responsibility for the work. That means review procedures, meeting the standards of their firm and profession. It also means you have only indirect control over the people doing the job.

Priorities of your auditing firm will often conflict with those of the corporation, as expressed through the project leader. Nothing is so costly, in time and money, as the resolution of conflicts among members of the team. That is especially true when a team member is accountable to another employer. Temporary, contract employees may be the best choice in some cases, particularly if the project manager is able to make the judgment calls in accounting presentation.

The ideal numbers person, like the ideal project manager, is someone for whom this assignment is a stepping stone for a career with the corporation. Numbers will come not only from the accounting function. Considerable information needs to be presented about the market, source of supply, competition, employees, and, often, technical matters. Being responsible for this part of the project teaches a lot about the corporation and its operating environment.

You may already have seen the potential for problems, in considering just these two members of the project team. The project leader is responsible to the chief executive and has been delegated top management authority, *for this project*. The numbers person reports to the project manager *for this project*. When it is over, the numbers person will have a permanent boss, perhaps you.

Career ambitions and anxieties can get in the way. That is one reason why you, and even the directors, must be informed all along the way. Pep talks will be necessary, as well as individual "and I really mean it" sessions. Everyone on the team will need to internalize the belief that their personal goals will best be met through a successful sale of shares.

Securities Lawyer

Many lawyers have done the legal work to comply with their state's laws for issuing corporate shares to a few inside shareholders. They have processed the paper for transferring shares from one owner to another. These do not a securities lawyer make. Securities lawyers are a rarefied breed. They come in subspecies of litigation, dealmaking (mergers and acquisitions), and financings. Within the subspecies of securities lawyers who specialize in financings, some may be most experienced in municipal bonds, and others in private placements or in international transactions.

You need someone who has been through a public offering registered under the federal Securities Act of 1933, on Form S-1 or Form S-18. The right person should be the lawyer who prepared the registration statement and filed it with the SEC. The job should have included following through to the effective date of the registration statement and the closing date of the offering.

Getting this position on the team filled may take time but it is often more important to the offering's success than even the project leader. Referrals can come from lawyers and accountants you know, and from management of corporations that have gone public. A preliminary screening will get you interviews with securities lawyers who have public offering experience. Before you meet with candidates for the securities lawyer's position, try to talk with some of their recent clients. Have them send you copies of prospectuses and other public documents these candidates have prepared.

Lawyers with specialized knowledge can be intimidating. Keep in mind that you are the client-to-be and the lawyer is a candidate to be your adviser and representative. You know your corporate shares are a good investment proposition for individuals. You have a plan for marketing those shares, one that will work. There is no law that says you cannot follow that plan. The only question is whether this securities lawyer is the right one to protect your corporation, its employees, and directors; a lawyer who will help you be fair to investors and make the process as smooth and effective as possible.

Most lawyers will start giving "free" advice during the interview process. This can be very helpful in telling you what quality of advice you will get when you start paying for it. For instance, a warning light should go on if you are encouraged to use the "intrastate" exemption from registration with the SEC. It is frequently considered too risky and certainly not an excuse for giving second-rate disclosure to prospective investors. The suggestion may signal the lawyer's insecurity and inexperience in dealing with federal securities laws. It may take a few interviews, but you will find a securities lawyer who is competent and willing to do it your way. You, of course, must commit to cooperate with the advice you get, perhaps after a few "why's" and "why not's."

Most securities lawyers come as part of a package in large to very large law firms. You may find a qualified person in a small firm or even practicing alone. Be blunt about asking whether the SEC would have more respect for a large, recognized firm name. Many law firms seem to make a division between the lawyers who bring the business in (the "rainmakers") and the lawyers who get the work out. Try to avoid the rainmaker and deal directly with the lawyer who will be in charge of your offering, but do not get below the partner level.

Large law firms often use a four-lawyer "team" when one or two lawyers will do. Listen particularly when you ask in the interview about who will actually do the work, whose face and voice will be part of the team. (Your project manager should be with you at the interview, to listen and take notes.) If you start hearing the "senior partner/junior partner/senior associate/backup senior partner" shuffle, be prepared to back off. Otherwise, you'll be paying to keep a lot of lawyers writing memoranda to each other. That multilevel approach can also result in billings for more time than was really devoted to your project. When a lawyer records time charges, it is very easy to log against someone else's project. Explanations after the offering are not much comfort. (More about this in Managing the Process.)

A final note on selecting the securities lawyer: It is far better to go with one who is light on experience than one who will not stay committed to seeing the job through. You are, in a direct offering, doing for yourself a job that has always "belonged" to securities firms. Most securities lawyers get a lot of work from securities firms, directly as clients or from referrals. You may run into "but you can't do it without an underwriter" or a smoother "let me introduce you to a really good investment banker." After all, that is probably the only way they have seen a public share offering done. And they will have friends and clients who are investment bankers.

Your lawyer may get a sharp reminder of these securities firms' connections from another partner in the firm. It is true that no major investment banker may be interested in your offering and that there is no local securities firm capable of doing it. Nevertheless, this is their historic turf. You should raise this issue specifically and be sure you feel satisfied with the assurances you get.

Advertising Agency

It is tempting to get caught up in the do-it-yourself mode and believe that word-of-mouth will sell your shares. Resist that temptation. Even if you are right, there is more to be gained than just getting these shares sold. You need an active trading market, continuous demand to keep the price up. There should be people already sensitized for the next offering. Advertising is the way your corporation will be introduced to strangers. It is the way information about your offering will be communicated. That kind of communication is an art. There are about 10,000 advertising agencies in the United States. Hundreds of them are capable of creating and implementing a campaign for selling your shares.

Creativity in advertising, always tough to identify, may come well after such qualities as willingness to cooperate with your lawyer and commitment to deliver quick turn-arounds on late, high pressure changes. In advertising as in legal work, you are hiring an individual or two, not an agency or firm. Personal reputation and chemistry are miles ahead of the organization's status and appearance in importance. It helps if you can use people you know and have worked with before. Get-acquainted time eats into the budget and schedule.

Using old hands can be a problem, too, however. If you have an advertising agency for the corporate product and image, they will be accustomed to a certain way of handling the relationship—who originates ideas, who makes decisions, who supervises costs and timing. Some will be able to handle a new way of doing things and some will not. You probably have experience with a general advertising agency, one which prepares and places advertising in any media. Even if you use a general agency, you may need to supplement their work with a specialist.

Because advertising people are often idea generators, they may take offense at being asked to implement other people's concepts. When it comes to marketing shareownership, we are all about equal in experience. Ideas can as likely come from the numbers person or the securities lawyer as from the advertising agency. It will be essential that the team members from advertising can accept limits from your securities lawyer and creatively include them. One offering was seriously delayed because a securities law official objected to a word used in the advertisement headlines. Qualities you will most need from people in advertising are cooperation, loyalty, efficiency, and even a dose of humility.

Direct Marketing Specialist

Advertising gets a message out there, to inform and persuade. But the results are indirect—some other marketing steps are needed before a sale is ready to close. Direct marketing tells the audience precisely how to respond. It gives a telephone number or furnishes a coupon to mail. There are mechanics in place to deal with responses to the specific campaign. Direct marketing (sometimes called "direct response marketing") has four elements in a share offering:

Proposition. The audience members are told that they will receive a prospectus if they respond to the advertisement; instructions are given about how to respond.

Response. There is a procedure for receiving and processing responses; systems are set and people are trained to evaluate and screen.

Fulfillment. A prospectus and related marketing materials are furnished, just as they were promised.

Conversion. Follow-up and closing methods are supervised, so that shares are sold in accordance with the securities laws and your own standards.

Direct marketing, particularly direct mail, is the most likely gap in a full-service agency. Many of them subcontract out the direct marketing component. Marketing shareownership relies heavily on direct mail and you may need to be forceful with your agency about getting a direct mail wizard as part of the team.

Market Research Experts

Your program will be more effective, and cost less, if you know where your target market is and how to reach it. That is the job of market research experts. You may be able to buy market research from your advertising agency. Most likely though, it would subcontract such research to a specialist. Insist on sending out your own requests for proposals and making your own contract with the market research firm. When you need market research, you want a direct relationship with the person doing it.

Market research can be a key to bringing all of your objectives together, that is to sell an acceptable percentage of your corporation at a fair price, to bring in shareowners who are likely to support your vision, and to complete the offering within a reasonable time and cost.

The answers you want from market research could include: Who are the people most likely to be interested in sharing ownership of your corporation? Which ones can also afford to buy corporate shares? What else do they have in common—knowledge that will tell you how to reach them. Where do they get their information? Whom do they trust for recommendations and endorsements?

Good market researchers will come up with far more useful questions, once they understand your purposes. Practical experience will guide them to identify market segments that can be reached and sold at an efficient cost. Their service will be interactive—you can fine tune your market selection as the program moves along. You are buying a member of the marketing team, not a research report.

Training Director

Your officers, directors, and employees are going to be carrying the corporate message to prospective shareowners. They could probably use some help in learning how to do that most effectively. Much of that training is defensive—you do not want to violate any securities laws, or have a shareholder later complain of having been misled. Everyone in the corporation will be educated to internalize the different "feel" arising from being publicly owned. They will at once become more guarded in what they can say about the corporation and more promotional in the way they express themselves about it.

It is helpful if the public offering training director is either drawn from within the corporation or will be on call after the offering. Public shareownership is a continuing part of corporate life and training directors will be needed to teach new employees about it and to explain how big corporate events should be handled in light of public shareownership. You may already have an employee practiced in training sales or production people. If not, you can see if someone already in the corporation has the interest and aptitude to do training.

Having in-house training directors means bringing someone in from the outside to "train the trainers" about public share offerings. This will be a short course in legal precautions and effective communication about selling shares. There will be role-playing sessions, with typical prospect questions and responses. And there should be an instruction booklet and written quiz. You will have a tape of the sessions to complete your compliance record.

Shareowner Relations Manager

Once your offering is sold, your corporation will always, ever after, be in the business of marketing its shares. Actual share offerings will occur only as you need to raise money or meet other objectives, but individual shareowners will have personal reasons to sell. That will mean a continuing need for market research and targeting market segments, for developing name recognition and favorable perception and for publishing information. All these mechanics are necessary to keep a constant demand for your shares. Your shareowner relations program helps produce a waiting list of interested people to buy those shares.

Building interest among prospective new shareowners is probably less important than preventing blocks of shares coming on the market because of uninformed selling. Shareowners who do not get current information tend to get nervous and sell. Worse, they rush to sell when there's bad news, creating sudden price drops, which cause other shareowners to panic and sell, and on and on.

Marketing shareownership is like marketing any other product. Your shareowner relations manager will prepare a plan, budget, and progress reports. The job will include market research and interaction with the securities firms that make a market in your shares. There can be coordination with other parts of the corporation, for cross-selling or cooperative promotions. Your investor relations manager will be most effective after being a part of the offering team, if not the team captain, then someone who has other marketing responsibilities.

A big part of the shareowner relations manager's job is to comply with the laws about disclosure of information. What requires a public announcement and when should it be made? How should the information be treated so that there is no selective disclosure to people who can trade before others know? When is it appropriate to keep a secret? Because of these concerns, many corporations have their investor relations officer report to the legal department or the chief financial officer. As a result, the investor relations program looks like something run by lawyers or accountants. Better to have the ideas and communications start somewhere else and be screened later for legal and accounting compliance.

If investor relations is to be a part of marketing, you will need clear, intelligent mechanics for legal and financial review of the regular communications with shareowners. A system must also be in place and tested for crisis management, so shareowners and prospective investors do not abandon the corporation from fear of the unknown in a catastrophe.

Shareowners who bought through your marketing programs will be natural allies in many marketing, political, and other corporate issues. Part of the investor relations job is to marshal those efforts effectively. With some careful supervision, you could let an investor relations person become a kind of advocate or ombudsman for shareowners— their pipeline to management. It may work well to have the investor relations function report directly to you or your top manager. That is, if the boss appreciates the importance of the job and takes a personal interest.

Information Systems Manager

This is the person with the knowledge to understand computer capabilities, the creativity to discover solutions, and the skill to manage a time-sensitive process. One of the first jobs is to make practical use of the market research conclusions about what sort of people comprise the shareowner market and how they can be reached. Another is to speed up the processing of legal and marketing materials and keep track of their results.

The step of building a prospect information file during the offering will flow into a data base for shareowners, prospective investors, and other interested persons. You can use a single personal computer for all the tasks, and the systems manager can be someone interested in expanding PC applications. This is one area where learning on the job is not so dangerous, as long as the competence and enthusiasm are there. Having the information systems manager as a part of the corporate staff is most helpful. It need not be someone who works full time in computer applications.

Outside Auditors

The accounting profession has had all the problems of a mature market for a generic service. The total number and size of public corporations has not been growing the way it did before the 1980s. The managements of public companies see the annual audit as a commodity—it has the same use and value from one well-known firm as from another. What happens when there is no perceived difference in quality is that competition is based on price, extra benefits, or personal relationships with the decision makers.

Extra benefits might include valuation or management consulting services. Keep it simple. Do not buy anything except an audit and their advice on accounting and tax issues. Those extra benefits will involve people outside the audit team, who have objectives that may just confuse things.

Selecting an auditor on the basis of friendship between the accounting firm partner and the corporate CEO or CFO is a bit touchy. Auditors are there to provide shareowners and others with an independent review and an opinion on the fairness of financial presentations. They must be objective. Better that you use your friend as an advisor and go to another firm for the audit. Personality is important, however. The audit partner can be practical and friendly, or stubborn and hostile. When dealing with the SEC and your securities lawyer, you need practical and friendly.

Public corporations have audit committees, usually made up of directors who are not employees. Those committees are supposed to pass on auditor selection and talk directly with the auditors about their work. You might as well have your directors pick an audit committee and let the committee get started by helping you pick the accounting firm for the public offering. There may be some accounting issues in your corporation that involve judgment as to how they are reflected in the financial statements. Your interview with audit firms can cover those.

Do not choose an auditor because of what he or she says will be allowed regarding issues to be resolved. Chances are, the people making those assurances can be overruled when their work is reviewed by others in their firm. This is likely to happen just when you are in a hurry to start selling shares. It is probably better to find a way of dealing with the issue that is not controversial, an accounting method that will come out the same with any auditor.

Like the securities lawyer and advertising agency, you want your auditor's references to tell you that they get the job done on time, within their cost quote and without causing a hassle.

Financial Printer

The day may come when any good printing company can handle a public offering. It is not here yet. Nor is desktop publishing ready to meet the time and accuracy demands of a prospectus. There are about ten financial printers in the United States. Most of them have gone out of business in the last few years and the large, national operations are down to just two, R. R. Donnelley & Sons Co. and Bowne & Co., with Merrill Corporation a distant third. Financial printers specialize, some exclusively, in printing public offering documents, shareowner proxy materials, and SEC filings. Financial printers exist because they provide a level of speed, accuracy, and personal service that other printers would never imagine. Some service becomes coddling, usually for the lawyer's benefit, but you can control that. Mostly, it is having the work done as quickly as humanly (and mechanically) possible, with an almost zero tolerance for error.

Word processing has reduced the dependency on printers that existed in the days of linotype, when every change had to be reset in metal using precomputer technology. You can manage the document-drafting process with your staff or your lawyer's. But it may still be too risky to try desktop publishing or using your local printer, no matter how many assurances you get.

Personal relationships and extra services will also be presented as a way to distinguish among financial printers. Here, the story is very different from the auditors. An audit is an audit, as far as the result is concerned. You want that "clean" opinion on your financial statements. How they get to that three-paragraph letter is not so important, since they are all competent and follow the same standards. But financial printers are selling a service, more than a result. They are managing a part of the process for you. By all means, choose one on the basis of how well you expect to get along and how much easier they can make the job for your people. Listen to the experience of your lawyer and accountant.

Price is critical. Financial printing is often the biggest single expense, even more than the lawyers and auditors. But, no matter how tightly you prepare your request for proposal and squeeze on their bid, you will still be at the printer's mercy in some surprise areas, such as last-minute copy changes and emergency turnaround time. You will have to rely on the experience of others and your own judgment on whether the printer will be fair and honest with you.

Closers

Closers are people who convert a show of interest into a sale. This will usually be done through an outgoing telephone call to someone who has requested and received a prospectus. The caller may be one of your employees, specially trained, or a securities broker from an outside firm. They deal with the natural tendencies of procrastination, indecision, and insecurity. At their best, closers just remove obstacles, so people can do what they really wanted to do. At their worst, they can get you in a lot of trouble.

Some prospective shareowners can express an interest, receive the written materials, and send in the order form with a check—all without any personal communication. Many individuals prefer to handle investments that way, to save time and their privacy. You are, however, probably not going to sell out your offering if you rely on the prospects who need no follow-up servicing. Most of us need to be moved to a close.

Before any outsiders can "sell" your corporation's shares, they and their employer must register with the SEC. But you can legally do a very low-key telephone follow-up through your own staff, with minimal securities law paperwork. Your employees just call to see if the prospectus was received, if there are any questions, and if the order form will be in the mail before the closing date. You cannot pay any commission to your staff, and you will need to provide them with training and supervision.

Should you consider using your own telemarketing staff, you will have some work to do with your securities lawyer to see what is possible and what safeguards you will need. You may have to register the corporation and the selected employees with state securities administrators.

If you go outside your corporation for closers, you will have to use brokers registered with the SEC and licensed by your state securities administrators. When you have a broker-assisted offering, where brokers sell shares to their own customers and prospects, it will operate apart from your own separate marketing program. There may be some duplication, but it should not be much. You can manage that through market selection and by giving your own direct marketing program a head start. You should then be paying commissions only on sales you probably could not have made without the broker.

Broker Closers.   Securities firms and their registered representatives have been used in direct offerings, made without an underwriting. Even Wall Street firms have let local brokers sell shares. But those have not been cases of using brokers to close leads generated by the corporation. Instead, brokers have sold shares to their own customers and prospects.

Brokers who have sold shares to their own leads have been paid a commission about equal to what a selling broker would get in an underwriting. (For instance, an underwriting commission of 8%, times 60% to the firm that employs the selling broker, would be 4.8%.) The firm then splits that with the broker under their own formula.

If you use securities brokers as closers for your own leads, then you will be turning over your prospect lists, generated from responses to your marketing program. The brokers will be telephoning or calling on those prospects, trying to convert them to a sale. There are registered broker-dealers that contract support services for independent financial planners. With tax shelter products mostly gone, many of the financial planners need something to sell individuals. You can learn about them from issues of *Financial Planning* magazine. For more information about brokers, buy or borrow a copy of *Securities Dealers of North America*, published twice yearly by Standard & Poor's. Look in the yellow pages and make some calls. Brokers are very telephone accessible. You can check on a firm's record of securities law violations through the regulatory agencies. A telephone inquiry service is furnished by the North American Securities Administrators Association at 1-800-942-9022.

There are some clear negatives in using securities brokers as closers. For one thing, the commission will likely be about 4% or 5%. That is what the selling commission would be in an underwritten share offering and that is about what securities brokers could make selling similar investment products. You can argue that it should be less because you are supplying the leads. And you may find some "freelance" brokers who will work for a smaller percentage.

Also, you have no control over what the broker has said to your new shareowner. Sometimes assurances are given about dividends, new business developments, or other surprises that come back to haunt you. Additionally, the relationship "belongs" to the broker, who is probably going to service it, giving advice on when to sell and buy another investment. If you decide you need brokers to be sure all the shares are sold, then the logical ones are your future market makers. They have the incentive to become experts on your corporation.

Market Makers

One day, the offering will be over. Your corporation will have hundreds or thousands of shareowners. Some of them will want to sell their shares. New people will wish to buy. Market makers match buyers and sellers. In a well-operated market, there are constant price offers available from sellers (ask price) and buyers (bid price). Transactions between sellers and buyers can take place in minutes. Results may be publicly displayed immediately, so everyone interested can see a trend in price or activity.

You will need to get a registered broker-dealer, someone in the market-making business, to handle your shares. A chance to make some commissions and meet some new prospects should be enough to motivate at least the two or three firms you need to keep the market liquid and honest. Your securities lawyer may be able to help you find a way for the corporation to cover a minimum level of income for the market making service.

When enough people are actively interested in buying and selling your corporate shares, brokers will simply become market makers, whether you arrange for it or not. But you need to know that there will be one or more ready to match buyers and sellers as soon as the offering is complete.

Your offering materials will have told investors that you expect a trading market to develop, so that they can sell their shares whenever they wish. You may have received preliminary clearance for having your share price quoted on the National Association of Securities Dealers Automated Quotation System (NASDAQ). Among other requirements,

NASDAQ needs to have two of its broker-dealer members say they will be market makers.

A specific individual in a brokerage firm near you is usually the place to go for a market maker. National firms may have some red tape that effectively prohibits their brokers from taking on this role, but many will permit it. A caution about selecting a market maker: Your corporation will be judged by what the broker says and how good a job the broker does. You will have almost no control over that. Before getting involved, it should be easy to learn the reputation of any local broker, and get to know the ones you would like to see dealing in your shares.

Sometimes a corporation will have only a few hundred shareowners, mostly people who want to hold on to their stock for the long haul. There may not seem to be enough activity for someone at a brokerage house. You might ask, "Why not have the president or someone else at the corporation keep a list of people who may want to sell and people who could be interested in buying, along with the prices they want?" Well, just ask your securities lawyer about that idea!

You will surely be advised that neither the corporation nor any of its officers or directors should ever act as a market maker for the corporate shares. If a buyer or a seller later has a choice between admitting a mistake in judgment or claiming to have been cheated, some will prefer to believe they were cheated—and set out to prove it in court.

There will always be something that people inside the corporation knew that people on the outside did not know. It may not have seemed important at the time. Or, maybe it was important but had to be kept secret for the corporation's benefit. Either way, it may look bad in hindsight.

If your shares just do not seem to trade, you have what is called a "thin" or "workout" or "by appointment" market. In fairness to your shareowners and corporate reputation, you will want to change that situation. A new offering would help, especially one aimed at attracting lots of buyers of smaller amounts—and not the "put it in the mattress and forget it" types. Maybe a stock dividend or stock split would free up some shares for trading.

It is best to have the market-making plans and commitments in hand before the initial public share offering. Investors need to know how they are going to get out before they ever get in.

Share Marketing Consultant

There have been direct share offerings for many years, usually born of frustration at not attracting an underwriter. Each one was like reinventing the wheel.

Until recently, most direct offerings registered with the SEC had been for interest-bearing notes, issued by finance companies. They were generally quite successful, and some of that learning curve has been transferred to direct offerings of corporate shares.

Direct marketing of shareownership really got started in the S&L business, back in its healthier days. Most S&Ls had been in the mutual form—technically owned by their customers—until they were allowed to convert to the shareowner form in the late 1970s. After some early experiments, conversion to the stock form really caught on in 1983. Customers of the institution were required to be given a chance to buy shares. Regulations permitted a "direct community marketing" to noncustomers as well. Since S&Ls had always been in the business of marketing savings accounts, many of them launched share marketing campaigns in addition to an underwriting, or even in place of an underwriting.

Some people gained an on-the-job education from these S&L public share offerings. Anyone who has been through more than one of these is a budding expert who could save you from making the same mistakes that others have already made. Beware of the awe factor, however. Someone who has experienced a direct share offering may cause you to feel ignorant and inadequate on the subject. You may be tempted to turn the whole project over to one of them—after all, they are the "experts."

Don't do it. Better to get along without any experienced consultant than to let them run the show and make decisions with which you will have to live. Would you let someone else market your most important product? What is more important than sharing ownership of the business you have created and nurtured?

If you can trust yourself to simply ask advice, listen, and make your own decisions, then by all means hire somebody who has been through a few direct share offerings. Pay your direct offering consultant on a basis related to their time. Agreeing to a "success fee" will make you wonder about the purity of their motives when giving you advice. Building a track record is enough of an incentive for them to give their best performance. Whether you hire a direct offering consultant or not, you will be able to get a lot of experienced advice from others on the team. Your securities lawyer, auditor, and financial printer will give you copies of documents from other offerings. Advertising agencies will build up some direct share marketing portfolios.

Time you spend developing talent within your corporation will not be wasted. Marketing shareownership is a continuous process. Your access to shareowner money—within a few weeks of deciding you would like to get it—will be a competitive advantage. It is too important to be left to outsiders.

Due Diligence, Endorsement, and Standby Commitments

Your job will be easier if someone independent is there to reassure investors—someone who (1) studies the investment proposition, (2) pronounces it a fair and promising one, and (3) commits to buy a major amount of the offering.

These are the roles performed by underwriters of shares a century and more ago. Together they say to individual investors: We have taken a hard look at this corporation and its share offering (due diligence); we find it a good investment (endorsement); we are willing to buy any shares that are not sold in the offering (standby commitment). Investors like the reassurance of believing that someone has done the investigation and exercised a judgment, just as they would do for themselves, if they had the time, skill, and access.

Your marketing program will respond to the insecurity individuals have about their ability to select shares without looking foolish. You will target markets of people who have a basis for making their own decision about your shares. And you will present information to them in a way that can help them make a decision. But it can still be useful to have an independent third party looking over your proposal to investors.

One role the securities underwriter and broker fulfilled was that of the scapegoat. A bad investment was their fault—"they're the experts. What do I know? I counted on them and they let me down." A good investment could still be a personal success—"my broker mentioned it and I studied the situation, used my own judgment. Turned out pretty well, if I do say so myself." A big part of dealing with the absence of this scapegoat role is to select target markets of people who have a personal frame of reference concerning your corporation—technicians who understand your business, residents of the community in which your corporation has a high profile, as well as your employees, customers, and suppliers.

Due diligence is a term born of the 1930s securities laws. When those involved in the offering are sued by a disappointed investor, they may defend themselves by proving they performed an investigation of the corporation and the information given investors with due diligence. The term has taken on general use as the process of checking on a corporation and the story told about it. That process is something different from the audit, which only results in an opinion by the auditing firm on the basic financial statements. While an audit opinion says that the balance sheet, income and related statements fairly present the company's financial condition and operating results, the due diligence investigation delves into such matters as management integrity, competitive position, product quality, and market reputation. It is comforting to prospective shareowners to know that someone with plenty of resources and clout has given the offering a thorough going over. Especially if that someone had a selfish reason for doing a good job.

Ideal for this job would be someone independent of the corporation who is willing to make a large investment in the share offering. This is the concept of "lead investor" used in most private share investments by venture capital funds. Endorsement by an established, competent outsider can be a major boost, even if the supporter is not investing in the shares. As with Underwriters Laboratory or federal meat inspection, it helps to know that the shares being sold have been passed on by someone whose job it is to do just that.

The government has been interposed as protector of the small investor. But the SEC makes it very clear that it does not endorse any public offerings. It doesn't even pass on the adequacy or accuracy of the written offering information. Its staff will make a series of editing suggestions for the prospectus, but the prospectus says, in big bold type on the cover, that it is a criminal offense to claim that the SEC has passed on anything.

Some state securities administrators are required to pass on whether the offering is "fair, just, and equitable," or some similar standard. But all the information that the civil servant has to make that judgment is the material filed by the corporation's lawyer. If a filing looks the way the examiner expects it to, and comes from a familiar law firm, that may be enough. Many states do not even look at offerings that are also filed with the SEC.

Bonds, commercial paper, and some preferred stock may carry ratings by Standard & Poor's or Moody's. Large corporations pay a fee for the rating, just as they pay the fees of independent auditors. Independence and objectivity are seldom questioned.

Mortgage securities and local government bonds can get insurance from companies with very deep pockets. Someday, there may be similar backing for corporate shares. For now, the best investors may hope for is that they share the risk with someone who is taking a big stake and has the ability to check things out.

For now, that endorsement factor may best come from

someone willing to make a standby commitment, to buy any shares not sold to the public. The endorsement could come from a venture capitalist, a large supplier, or other corporate ally. Their commitment agreement could give them a discounted price for the shares left unsold in the public offering. For a larger discount, they might agree not to sell any of the shares for three years or so.

Your standby commitment could come from a group of investors. But they should not be drawn from people who are expected to be regular investors. You will need all the "big hitters" you can get to build the bandwagon enthusiasm of an offering that is selling fast. Terms of this standby commitment would be prominently described in the prospectus and other offering materials. It might even be subject to having a minimum number of shares sold in the public offering, to at least enough shareowners to make a trading market.

A tool popular in Japan is to sell shares to large investors at a discount from the offering price, provided they agree not to sell the shares for a period of three years or so. These arrangements must be disclosed in the offering, and the discount must be fair. This means that some investors, who are able and motivated to study the proposition, have agreed to be stuck with a significant share investment for some time.

You may have no trouble selling shares in your corporation to several hundred individuals without any due diligence and endorsement by an outsider. Perhaps you can tolerate the risk of unsold shares without having a standby commitment. A constituency may exist that has an enthusiasm that will leap over doubts. Your employees, customers, and community could be enough. Just be sure that market research has confirmed your intuition.

PROPOSALS AND CONTRACTS

Your first big action step will be requesting proposals and turning the responses into contracts. Through this process, you will assemble your team and set the tone for relationships during the whole project. The proposal process will also answer questions before they come up and clear away the sources of conflicts that can ruin timing, budget, and even the end result.

The process begins with a request for a proposal. Rather than a formal document, it will usually be a letter, telephone conversation, or meeting. You will explain what you want from your financial printers, market research and ad agency, as well as your lawyers, auditors, and consultants—then they will tell you whether they can do it and how much it will cost. In some cases, you will send only very general requests for a proposal. Your securities lawyer, for instance, will not need to be told what steps are involved in regulatory clearances and protection from shareowner litigation. You will describe objectives with lawyers, accountants, and consultants. You will describe your project management, the timing, and the way team members are to report and get approvals. Then your professionals will be asked to explain their services, why they are best qualified for the job, and how you will be charged.

There are good reasons why you do not want to negotiate the way in which your accountant will do the audit or the way your securities lawyer will deal with the SEC. Beyond wasting your time and theirs, you may lose your right to rely on them as the experts. They have professional standards of competence, and you are paying to see that they adhere to those standards. Do not let them off the hook by making judgments that should be theirs. You can, however, have these professionals describe the frequency and method by which they will report to you as the project moves along and when you will be asked to make decisions.

In your request for a proposal, you can explain that your selection is based on many factors beyond price and credentials. Ask for creative suggestions about how the offering can be made more effective, and the cost of the elements that those suggestions would add to your specifications. Fee discussions are always more pleasant, and much less costly, when they occur going into a project, rather than coming out of it. In talking about fees, ask your professionals to explain a little about how they propose to do the work, at least in terms of the way the job will be staffed.

Beware of paying for on-the-job training and helping to meet billable hour minimums for back-up people. You can ask a few "but do you really need" questions. Watch out for remarks about "limiting the scope of our engagement," or some such comment. You could get set up for excusing less than professional performance, because you insisted on cutting back on what professional advisers said was necessary. Their proposal letter should assure you that they will adhere to professional standards for this kind of work. When you understand what results you can expect, it then needs to be clear how much you will pay and when.

You and the professionals have a clear conflict when it comes to fees. They generally get paid on the basis of the time it takes and the billing rates of the people they put on the job. It is hard to guess how much time will be involved, and at what hourly rate. Who takes the risk of it being more or less than expected—you or their firm?

Not you.

If you have been able to talk with your counterparts who have gone public, you will probably have heard some horror stories about professional fees. When it gets into the heat of the last few weeks of the project, you will be ready to say something like, "I don't care what it costs, just get it done." That is not a favorable time to be making cost decisions.

Will you be able to get a proposal that covers every possible cost overrun? Of course not. Will you be able to protect your corporation from paying a lot more than really necessary? Probably. It helps to remember that you hire individual professionals, not their firm. Proposals should say who will be in charge and who will do the work. An impressive firm name may be useful in creating first impressions among regulators and even some investors. It supposedly stands for professional competence and character. But you cannot look a law firm or advertising agency in the eye—you need to be comfortable with another human being.

There are ways to have proposals from professionals be

as thorough and comparable as you can get. One is to get ideas from each candidate about what you should be looking for, how you can best protect your corporation and its future shareowners. Another safeguard is to hire a person just for the purpose of helping you select someone else in the same profession. Find a securities lawyer who is not a candidate but who can give you the benefit of experience from the inside. Similarly with a retired auditor and with a veteran of the advertising agencies. They can help in preparing your interview checklist and proposal review.

You are the one who meets with representatives of the final candidates for lawyers, advertising agencies, accountants, and financial printers. They need to be impressed with your personal involvement, and you want to take their measure. Your project manager will be with you, taking notes and covering any remaining items from your checklist. When you have selected a proposal, and have then negotiated it into an acceptable revision, simply sign it as revised. That is the contract. They prepared it. It is on their letterhead, signed with their firm name. They should have no excuse for getting out of it.

Requests for proposals sent to financial printers, market research companies, and others are a very different proposition from the lawyers, auditors, and consultants. You want their proposals to tell you exactly what they are going to do, along with the timing and cast of characters for each item. You can also ask them to suggest and price innovations and shortcuts. Tell them that this creativity will be a factor in awarding the contract. Part of what you will have received in the proposals from your lawyer and consultant is their assistance in picking the other outsiders for your team. Their experience can help predict the trouble spots and can also help put together clear specifications for the bidding process. You would be amazed at how much information competing vendors will provide in tightening up specifications.

Financial printers, for instance, can be as maddeningly frustrating as they are indispensible. Some of them have had a rule of thumb, at least for the busy times: the final printing bill should average three times the price quoted. Such seemingly harmless words as, "Each author's alteration—$30," can translate into many thousands of dollars in cost overruns.

This example shows another benefit from detailed proposals. Financial printers do not cheat. Their prices are reasonably related to their costs. What they usually do not contribute is advice on how *not* to use their services. Those "author's alterations" are usually made by your securities lawyer or your auditors. In the ideal world, copy never gets to the financial printer until it is final, Final, FINAL. Then any alterations are corrections of "printer's error," at no charge to you. Your request for a printing proposal can call for any alteration charges to be approved by your project manager before the changes are made. This arrangement can also be confirmed in the lawyer's and accountant's proposal letters, so that they are on notice that the printer must clear changes with the project manager.

Financial printers get many of their jobs by coddling the securities lawyers and accountants who refer them to clients. Who does not like to be pampered if someone else is paying for it? Proposals and contracts should squeeze out most of this luxury service.

Complete and airtight proposals are much to be desired. But they are not the sole basis for making your selections for the team. You want people with whom you feel comfortable and confident. You can also get a lot of service that is not in the proposal, if suppliers are motivated to provide something extra.

For example, financial printers are a good source of extra help. Some have staff who know more than most of us could ever learn about how to make printed materials simple and elegant. Financial printers will also have worked with many of the securities lawyers and accountants who do public offerings (and often know more about the technical requirements of signatures and number of copies for SEC filings). And they have lots of copies of documents similar to what you will be producing.

You want the proposals you receive from each group of

competitors to be comparable with each other, so you can make a direct analysis of relative quality and cost. But your decision will include your judgment on such soft factors as creativity, team spirit, and commitment.

SCHEDULE AND BUDGET

Your corporation is prepared for public shareownership, and you have selected the people to do the offering. Now you need the framework that will help them work together like a practiced team. Marketing your shares directly is a simple idea. But actually carrying it out is a complex process. One task must often be completed before another can begin. Money has to be carefully conserved. And the job all must be done within a few weeks. Most important, you need to run your business with as little distraction as possible. It is as if your team had to design, test, manufacture, and market a major new product. That is, in fact, just what you are doing, and you have very limited time and money for the job.

Time limits are set by the SEC rules for a prospectus, the information booklet that describes your corporation and the share offering. Financial information must be brought up to a certain date before the offering is over. Delay can mean redoing hundreds of hours of work, usually at a much less productive morale level.

Facts about your corporation change every day. The more time that goes by, the less accurate will be the picture drawn in the offering materials and the more likely that something will have happened that investors ought to know. If the schedule is not tight enough, or someone on your team is not keeping up, you can get into a Catch-22 situation: Something gets out of date in the offering materials. By the time that section gets revised, you cannot use it because it conflicts with another part. When that part is changed, something else is stale. It can go on and on, and people start getting discouraged.

Scheduling a public share offering is similar to the critical path analysis used for other complex projects. There are many separate tasks, each beginning on its own path. Each needs to intercept another path at just the right moment and go on to the next juncture, until they all have come together at closing. Some things can go on in parallel. Others must wait for another step to be completed.

Typical schedules will have three columns: one to describe the assignment, another for the name of the person responsible for it, and the third for the date when it should be completed. Your information systems manager may suggest some more effective formats. In the precomputer days schedules looked like this one (see Table 5.1). Responsibility for each step is placed on an individual, rather than a title or a firm name. That helps avoid genuine confusion, as well as any buck-passing games.

Part of the project manager's job is to monitor the schedule, with all the sensitivity and effectiveness possible. Your information systems manager will help work out a method to update and distribute the schedule. Imaginative programming can find a way to signal when steps are to be done.

There will usually be some who do not take the schedule seriously. They may test your commitment by letting something slide past a due date. It is at that moment when you must demonstrate for all involved that your project manager acts with your complete support.

Budgeting should be much easier than scheduling. If the proposal stage has been well performed, there will be no major open costs. If there are any overruns by outside ven-

Table 5.1. Public Share Offering Schedule

Person Responsible	Step to Be Completed	Completion Date: 1990
Rollins	Approve final schedule	January 4
Murdoch	Provide requests for prospectus data to all	January 5
Weiland	Schedule focus groups, telephone interviews	January 5

dors, the requests for proposals should have made it clear that they will be the vendor's responsibility.

Budgets and schedules generally assume that everything goes perfectly. Of course, nothing ever does. The biggest additional costs are caused by slippages in the schedule—when something must be redone because it became outdated. Once your project is off schedule, or over budget, accountability becomes fuzzy and other slippages occur, creating a domino effect. Your project manager will know where the shortcuts can be made, so that you have some places to make up time and offset expense when you need to. Your budget and schedule are not padded, but places will have been built in where time and money can be saved with the least sacrifice.

Lawyers and accountants have the scope of their work largely defined by legal requirements, and there is not much you can do to change that. But the selection of marketing media, and the intensity of its use, is almost entirely your choice. For advertising expenditures, there is the old adage: "I know half the money is wasted, but I can never figure out which half." That will be less so with your marketing program because you can test results and then adjust to accommodate. But, when you begin your budget, you can only guess. Much of the spending in your program is discretionary. You can begin with an amount to spend and create a marketing program to fit it.

Setting a Budget Total

One rough way to build a marketing budget is simply to plan spending a certain percent of what you expect to raise through the offering. Your team then designs a marketing program to squeeze the most results out of the dollars available. There are some useful guidelines for what a reasonable marketing cost would be.

State securities administrators often set a limit on expenses they will permit for securities sold in their state. If that limit is 15% of the total offering proceeds, you will want to leave some margin for surprises in your budget, setting

Table 5.2. Budget Model

For a $5 million offering, 12% total budget	$600,000
Legal, accounting, financial printing, and other predictable costs are expected to be	$200,000
That would leave, for all marketing costs	$400,000
If securities brokers are used for closing, and half the sales go through them, that means commissions of about 5% of $2.5 million, or	$125,000
There remains, for other marketing costs	$275,000

your limit at 12% or so. Also, you can use an underwriter's fee schedule as a guide for your marketing budget. A securities firm underwriting a $10 million offering would charge at least 8%, plus some stock purchase options. Without putting a price on the options, and leaving out the effect on pricing your shares caused by an underwriting, that translates into an $800,000 marketing budget. Legal, accounting, and financial printing costs will be additional, and about the same for an underwriting as a direct marketing.

For how a budget might be constructed, starting with a percentage for total expenses, and working back to get an amount for marketing costs, see Table 5.2.

Accounting for Share Offering Proceeds and Expenses

Offering expenses are subtracted from the proceeds of the shares sold. Then the net proceeds are added to the share-owners' equity section of the balance sheet. Receipts from the sale of corporate shares do not go through the income statement. Neither do the expenses related to the sale. The only exception is when an offering is abandoned—not just postponed for a month or so, but called off or put on hold indefinitely. Then the amounts actually expended on the offering are treated as expenses of the period in which the offering was abandoned. When an offering is concluded, its costs never go through the earnings statement. For tax purposes, it might be nicer if offering expenses could be written off against current income. For reporting earnings as the results of your regular business operations, the deduction from proceeds method is a more accurate picture.

To sell your stock, you will need to promote your corporate image. Benefits from that image advertising will naturally affect your customers, community, and employees. Auditors have not yet suggested any allocation of the amount spent between the offering and general expenses. That presents an opportunity to have a major image promotion without charging the costs against operations. They are offset against the proceeds of the offering.

Blending with Other Marketing Programs

People who use your products or services may be targeted as a market for your corporate shares. It could certainly make sense for you to blend your share offering and product marketing messages. There could even be tie-in programs. In preparing your budget, you may see some opportunities to coordinate with other marketing activities. Any crossover benefits, however, are not worth endangering the primary purpose of completing a share offering and acquiring a hospitable and helpful shareowner family.

MARKET RESEARCH

Schedules and budgets are completed before the rest of the work is really underway. They will surely be revised, but they are a front-end step in the project. Market research also begins early and is continuously revisited. Your market research component can be similar to the use of pollsters in an election campaign. A lot of work is done and some conclusions are drawn before the marketing program is designed. But even then, market research continues through the preparation, testing, and even the final offering days.

There is very little hocus-pocus to market research. Much of it is just testing and confirming your own instincts. You need answers you can rely on for questions like these:

Who is most likely to buy our shares?

What media will reach them cost-effectively?

Which messages will work best with each group?

Tools of market research include matching published demographic information with the facts about your corporation, conducting telephone interviews, and running focus groups. It can all be very academic, with results expressed in statistical probabilities. But when it is conducted and interpreted by skilled practitioners, market research can save you far more money than it costs.

You and the people who help you run your business are the best ones to make decisions about your shareowner marketing program. There is the temptation to let decisions be dictated by market research, because its results can be quantified and thus carry an air of measured certainty. If your collective intuition conflicts with the scientific results of market research, don't be afraid to go with your hunch.

Through market research, you can begin living with your new shareowners before you ever start marketing to them. Who are the people who should want to own shares in your corporation? What are their interests, motivations, and dreams? How have they spent their extra dollars so far—expensive cars, lottery tickets, getaway trips? What do you share with these people, other than an interest in your corporation? Can you be comfortable in their heads and hearts for a few minutes?

Imagining answers to questions like these is an exercise for the corporate founders. For a few months, a top priority for your contemplative time can be understanding the personalities of your future shareowners. You can then be better prepared to make policy decisions for the marketing program.

DESIGNING YOUR MARKETING PROGRAM

You have made a decision to share ownership with the public, at least representatives of certain market segments of the public. Your sense of timing says to do it now. You have put together your project team. A working schedule and budget are ready. Market research has suggested your target markets and the media you need to reach them. It is time to design your marketing program.

Individuals are not going to (1) get the urge to own shares, (2) initiate their own information gathering, (3) make a decision to buy, and (4) complete a purchase—all by themselves. The urge, the information, the decision, and the action will happen because of a marketing program— one with tools for packaging, advertising, servicing, and closing. A share marketing program begins with packaging—the way you are presenting what you have to sell, your investment proposition.

Your Investment Proposition

Somewhere there is a sentence that tells a person why he or she wants to share ownership in your corporation. It is an invitation that makes sense and makes an individual want to know more. In ten words, more or less, your one truthful sentence will tell that person what the corporation is and what is in it for that individual to buy some shares. If your investment proposition does not fit in about ten words, perhaps the business is not ready for public shareowner-ship. You may be better served shopping for capital with people who can listen to the whole story over lunch, and then take home your business plan to study. Venture capitalists. Wealthy acquaintances. People who can invest an amount of money that will justify the time you each will have to spend.

That certainly does not mean your business must be simple. It can be extremely technical and complex. But its money-earning potential must be clearly apparent to your shareowner profile.

Preparing the First Draft

Now you know what you have got to sell. Early market research and your own intuition have suggested some natural markets for your shares. The schedule and budget are your limits in time and money. Someone should now be able to come up with a draft of the marketing program. That first draft can come from your advertising agency, your marketing consultant, or someone on your staff. It is not so important that it be a great job, because it is only a beginning. But, for the team's effectiveness, it can be really important who writes the first edition.

Human nature will make some market researchers want to design your marketing program. Advertising creative types will believe they are the ones to do that. Securities lawyers may see themselves in the mastermind role. Try not to let any one of them grab it and run. Once they do, you may lose the enthusiasm of everyone else on the team. Once an individual has emerged as the author of the marketing program, that person becomes the logical candidate to take the blame if all does not go well. And if it is a huge success, the "author" will try to take all the credit. This puts the team captain and everyone else into a mood for giving less than their best effort. Everyone needs to "own" the marketing plan. The whole team needs to participate in drafting its elements. The integrated program should be approved by consensus—no dissenters or nonparticipants to say "I told you so" or "if you'd only asked me first."

That first draft marketing program should come from someone whose ego can afford to have the draft torn to pieces, again and again. Even if it is perfect at the time, new information will mean it should be changed. It would be a bad idea to have the securities lawyer draft a marketing plan, even if your lawyer shows a great flair for marketing. Any time someone suggested a change, the lawyer could protect pride of authorship through comments like, "Oh, the SEC would never allow that," or "But that would really expose us to a shareowners' suit." Even worse would be the securities lawyer who compromised legal advice for personal ambitions and pride. How can the same person test the boundaries of propriety and, at the same time, give opinions on where these boundaries are?

Suppose you prepare the draft by yourself, or together with your project manager. Who else on the team is going to tell you it has defects, even indirectly, by making suggestions for major changes? If someone did, could you bring yourself to acknowledge that it needed all those changes? How would that affect your relationship with each of the team members?

You may find that consensus drafting is the best way to do the marketing plan. One approach would be to have the advertising agency representative be the facilitator in a morning session during which a rough outline is drafted and the next steps are assigned. Then the facilitator can gather comments, incorporate the results of assigned tasks, and distribute a draft. The next round can be with the full team divided into smaller groups to deal with particular areas. Eventually, everyone signs off on a working draft. However the marketing program is first drafted, it will be changed continuously throughout the project, as events bring new facts and new inspirations.

PRICING THE SHARES

When you were deciding whether to share ownership with the public, you estimated how much money you wanted to bring into the corporation and about what percentage ownership you would be willing to sell. The market research and advice you have received during the preparatory stage may have modified these numbers.

How much you raise in the offering relates directly to the percentage ownership you are willing to sell to the new shareowners. If you want to retain 70% after the first offering, the question is whether you can raise the capital you need by selling 30%. Valuing your company for an initial public offering is very different from valuing when you want to sell the entire business. It also involves different considerations from those in a private sale of an interest in the business. Shareowners in a public company have no role in management, but they have a liquid market in which they can sell their shares at any time.

You have to be satisfied that your offering price is fair to you and the new shareowners. You also need to know that it is a price prospective investors will be willing to pay for your shares, rather than buying shares of another corporation, or using their money for some other purpose. Be willing to price at an "introductory bargain." If you sell shares now, and they have continuing increases in trading price, it will help you sell shares in the next offering at a "quality premium."

Corporate valuation is the subject of many articles and entire books. Specialists charge large fees for preparing thick valuation reports. Their methodologies have long mathematical formulae and elaborate justifications. But at the bottom of any fair market value is a guess at what price would be reached between a buyer and a seller.

Market Prices for Shares
of Comparable Companies

For new corporate share offerings, most valuations are based on a "peer group" of other corporations. The ideal is to find companies that are just like yours in every respect—except that they are already publicly traded. In theory, what price the trading market sets for those stocks predicts what investors would pay for shares in your corporation. Once a peer group is assembled, the process is like reverse engineering a competitor's product. The market prices of their shares are taken apart, to see how they relate to such factors as revenue, earnings, and cash flow (all for the past and projected future). The prices are also compared with various categories of assets, liabilities, and equity.

These results are then given something called a "sensitivity analysis" or similar jargon. That is, attempts are made to compare the quality of customer base, management, market share, supply relationships, and other factors that should make one business more valuable than another.

Price-earnings (P/E) ratios are the most common in comparative valuations. If your corporation and its peer group have all been earning a profit for a few years, and have about the same growth rate, then P/E ratios will do nicely for your decision-making purposes. P/E ratios vary considerably over time. For the S&P 500, the stock price times average earnings has averaged 14.4 since 1926. But the ups and downs of the stock market have pushed P/E ratios to nearly 20 and to only about 7, within a few months. P/E ratios that are based on past earnings only work for companies that have long ago completed their period of rapid growth. Entrepreneurial corporations usually have to project future earnings to come up with a price. For a ratio based on past performance, they have to use a substitute for price earnings, such as price revenue, or even price to projected revenue.

From the investors' point of view, the stock price is based on their expectation of what they will receive back from holding and eventually selling the stock. Then they have to consider the risk that their expectation will not come true. One way to approach that is to estimate the future cash flow into the corporation and then use a discount rate to put a present value on that stream of cash.

Discounted Cash Flow

The theory behind this method of value is that the cash generated by a corporation will benefit the shareowners, one way or another. In the very long run, the return could be in cash dividends. It could all come at once, if the corporation were acquired for cash. More likely, a shareowner will realize a cash return by selling shares into the trading market. The buyer will pay a price based on a current estimate of future cash flow. Discounted cash flow means estimating how much cash the business will generate and then dividing that by a percentage rate of return. It cuts through all the accounting standards that are involved in calculating "income."

"Cash" means the money left over from receipts after paying the bills. Because it measures the entire life of the corporation, a cash-flow analysis treats major capital outlays, such as a new building, the same way as everyday operating expenses, such as paying the utility bill. There is no attempt to spread the amount over some estimated useful life, as with the accounting practices of amortization and depreciation.

On the other side of the equation is the rate of return investors would require for shares in your corporation. That starts with simple rent on the use of their money, forgetting any risks at all. Usually that has been between 2 and 3% per year.

To the rental rate, we add the return required to cover the general risks of having money tied up for a long period. These include investors' expectations about the decline in value of the dollar through inflation and international monetary exchange rates. In the United States, most of us do not add a factor for possible revolution, expropriation, or occupation.

The third element of the discount rate covers the particular risk of seeing your corporation achieve the expected cash flow.

Putting these three components together is seldom done in pure analysis. Instead, we use surrogates. The interest yield on 30-year U.S. Treasury bonds becomes the measure of the first two elements—rent plus general economic risk. Rent on money, and the price for risking devaluation, is the rate of return we would require on U.S. Treasury obligations. They are generally considered to have no risk of loss or delayed payment.

For the risk of owning shares of American corporations generally, we look at the average dividend rate plus price appreciation for blue-chip stocks. That has run from 4 to 7% over Treasury bond yields.

Your corporation will be considered a higher risk than the blue-chip market. As a consequence, your corporation's price will fluctuate more than blue chips do, both up and down. That relative volatility is its "beta." You can figure your beta by looking at relative price fluctuations of your peer group of publicly traded companies that are most like yours. If those shares are twice as volatile as the market, their beta is two. These elements all come together by multiplying the equity risk premium times your beta, then adding that to the current Treasury bond rate.

For instance, stocks may be returning 6% more than Treasury bonds. With a two beta, your shares need a 12-point premium. At an 8% yield on Treasury bonds, investors will value your shares to get a 20% annual rate of cash return. This seems like a lot of detailed academic theory. But your board of directors will be setting the price on the portion of the corporation you will offer to the public. They need a record of rational analysis to support that value.

Price per Share

When you have decided on the offering amount and the percentage ownership that you are selling, you are ready to set a price per share for the public offering. In an underwriting, you would negotiate this price with the investment banker. Early on, the number of shares would have been fixed, so last minute price reductions would usually mean getting less money for giving up the same number of shares. When you market directly, the arithmetic is a little different. You decide on a price per share that you believe is best for the investor prospects you have selected. Then you divide that number into the total dollar amount you expect to raise. After a little rounding, that will tell you the number of shares to be offered.

Price Influences Perception. The art is in coming up with a price per share that creates the most favorable image. Folklore has it that an initial public offering priced at over $20 per share is intended for a sophisticated market of institutions and the wealthy. The price conveys that this is an established business not subject to rapid price movement, up or down. In analysts' terms, it is a "low beta" investment, one that will move closely with the stock market averages.

In the $15 to $20 range, shares represent a higher expected price fluctuation, because the company is young. However, it is probably marketing an established product, so the risk has to do with its ability to gain market share and be profitably managed. Wall Street investment bankers will often push for an initial public offering price of between $10 and $15. Since established corporations usually have trading price ranges of $30 to $60, there is clearly room for seeking that level. A single-digit price has been looked on by Wall Street as a second-class position, a corporation that would not likely make it onto the NYSE listing—perhaps an interesting little stock, but not for proper investment portfolios.

Below $5 a share puts a corporation in the penny stock category. That is the high-risk, double-your-money-in-a-week class. If a price gets into that game, it might as well be set at 10 cents and really catch the speculative fever. Between $5 and $10 may work best for a direct share marketing. There is still some sentiment for buying at least 100 shares, and it may still be cheaper to sell a "round lot" (100 share multiples) in the trading market than an "odd lot."

Pricing your shares becomes another challenge for market research and intuition.

MANAGING THE PROCESS

You have selected a manager and assembled a team. Now they need to manage the process to success, while causing as little disruption as possible to the ongoing business. Such tools as newsletters, CC's, and meetings, daily progress reports, incentives, and recognition are used in direct stock offerings to smooth the path.

Newsletters, "CC's," and Meetings

Everyone on your team needs to know what is going on with the whole project, as frequently as possible. Other people involved—employees, brokers, the staff at your advertising agency, and so forth—should get reports at least weekly during the thick of the campaign. This can be done with catchy newsletters or whatever is most effective.

Visual communications within the team are mostly read-and-throw-away. Once the offering is over, no one needs to keep anything, except a legal compliance record and a file of prototypes for the next offering. Sending "CC's" (copies of written work product) can keep everyone informed and give them a chance to contribute, without making a ceremony of it. Showing, by the symbol "CC:" at the bottom of the document, who has received copies, can emphasize the team nature of the endeavor.

Meetings are particularly treacherous in a direct share offering. Things move too quickly to keep everyone current on what the rest of the team is doing. And you certainly do not want the diffused responsibility of decision making by consensus. Decisions need to be made by the person responsible for the task, with the knowledge and approval of the project manager.

Daily Progress Reports

Your major contractors are the ad agency, lawyers, accountants, and financial printer. Their work is described in proposals and they operate largely independent of supervision by your project manager. This can mean nasty surprises, not only in cost overruns but in conflicts, duplication, and waste. These contractors can keep logs or diaries of what they do each day, who does the work and how much was spent that day in time and money. They need this for their internal purposes, although that is not any guarantee that they always do it. Insist on it. Make it a part of your request for proposal. Your project manager will collect and study these daily progress reports and quickly follow up with questions or directions.

Incentives and Recognition. You cannot pay commissions for selling stock unless you have complied with extensive SEC broker-dealer regulations. This means you should stay away from any compensation arrangements that could be mistaken for commissions.

You will be asking people to make a special effort, work extra time, and take on some difficult assignments. They need some incentives and some recognition for a job well done. In addition to rewarding contribution, there is benefit from simply keeping up a level of awareness and excitement among the team and all the corporate employees.

Some corporations have taken a very conservative approach and kept awards entirely apart from performance. They had prizes for contests, such as guessing the time when the first stock order would be received, or the number of shareowners there would be after the offering, or the number of prospectus requests a particular ad would generate. Other companies have tied incentives to performance, not to results. The number of follow-up telephone calls made in a day, how many people showed up at an investment seminar—all without regard to whether shares were sold.

ELEMENTS IN A MARKETING PROGRAM

You can organize your marketing program around the steps that get you from where you are to your goal of being a corporation with public shareownership and a trading market. Marketing programs answer such questions as these:

1. Who are the affinity groups to attract?
2. What media do you select to reach them?
3. What will the message look and sound like?
4. How do you enlist allies in the campaign?

5. What is the followup system?
6. Who will close the sales?
7. What do you do after the offering is over?

Your Affinity Groups

An early job you can assign yourself is to describe the kinds of people you would choose to have as fellow shareowners. At the same time, you can list the types you would rather avoid. In this exercise, you do not need to factor in what is possible or even what may be difficult. Just let your imagination run free in creating a profile of your perfect team of fellow shareowners.

Shareownership is about more than getting money into the corporation. You can gain ambassadors of good will, loyal enthusiasts who will carry the corporate message. Your ability to sell shares in the future will be affected by the market experience of your first shareowners. With an eye to the future trading market for the shares, you will want to have a blend of investment motives. It would be disastrous if most investors were expecting to sell within the first few weeks, whether they gained or lost. But it is nearly as unfortunate if all the buyers put their shares away to be forgotten for a few years.

You need some buyers with short-term motives to get a market going. Those with long-term objectives keep the supply from overwhelming demand. Intermediate-term investors assure that the market will not dry up, that a moderate price rise will bring some shareowners into the market.

You will probably be parting with about 30% of the total ownership as a result of the offering. Future sales of shares, either by the company or to diversify your own holdings, will further dilute your control. The more broadly the remaining shares are spread, the more likely you will be safe from a takeover.

Beyond trading market considerations, your shareholder profile can be designed around other parts of your business. It pays to have shareowners in positions to boost the corporate business, within legal rules and ethical standards. Leaders in your local community can be valuable supporters. Customers and suppliers are natural dual-motive shareholders. It is in their self-interest that your business prosper and grow. As investors, they have the advantage of knowing your people and products, and having a continuing window on your operations.

Profile of the Ideal Shareowner Mix

When you prepare requests for proposals to market researchers and direct marketing specialists, you can include your description of the ideal shareholders. These firms will temper your view with their experience on how best to sell the shares. This shareholder profile exercise may influence your overall business plan. Once you have committed to using public shareowners to finance the corporation, you need to have a business that will attract individual investors. Some bending to shareowner appeal is certainly ethical and good business planning—for instance, keeping the lines of business as clean and simple as possible and choosing directors who will raise the confidence level of shareowners. In designing the ideal shareowner mix, you can emphasize various attributes that you would like in your buyers, in addition to simply selling the shares. Such positives as boosters, deep pockets, loyalists, and even "plankton" might be included.

Boosters. One of the things that has been learned from direct share marketings is that everyone does not buy corporate shares just for profit. They may say that is their reason, and even convince themselves intellectually. But deep down, they really always wanted to be a part of some quality they find in your corporation. Employees are motivated to own a share of the place where they work. Avid users of your products or services may want to strengthen their ties through shareownership. Neighbors in your community might want to be part of the local success story. Key to the boosters is their dual motive for being a shareowner.

Loyalists.   You will probably still own most of the shares, even after the first public offering. Maybe after the second and third. At some point in the life of almost every entrepreneur comes the day when personal shareownership goes below 50%. Even while you own a majority of the shares, it is nice to have other shareowners in your corner, giving management the benefit of the doubt, sending in their proxies all voted for management recommendations, and not selling when results are disappointing. These are the loyalists.

Deep Pockets.   However confident your team is about selling all the shares offered, you need some major buyers— deep pockets—to get the ball rolling. Most offerings also need the deep-pocket investors to close the gap at the end of the offering period. These investors may have to be treated differently from all the rest of the shareowners. Some become directors of the corporation. There may even be arrangements about a price difference in exchange for an agreed holding period. Of course, these arrangements must be made in advance and described in the offering documents.

"Plankton."   At the base of the "food chain" of corporate shareowners are those who will sell a few shares whenever the price starts to get higher than they think it is really worth. Some of them will buy more shares when the price is below their perception of value. These are the shareowners who make it possible for your corporation to have a real trading market. Do not be insulted that they do not plan to stay with you forever, through thick and thin. Turnover, within a fair price range, is good for the corporation's ability to attract new shareownership. It also provides the liquidity that will let major investors sell a few shares now and then to get back some of their cash investment.

Your profile of the ideal shareowners can probably be sifted into multiple layers. There will be individuals who own at least $100,000 worth and are almost an advisory board to you. At the other end will be investors who intend to sell their 100 shares within a year, or sooner if the price moves sharply up or down.

Part of this imagining process will be visions of the shareowners you would like to avoid, to the extent you can:

Speculators. These could turn your trading market into a roller coaster ride;

Curiosity Seekers. These just want a few shares so they have access to information and attention; and

Disrupters. These are antagonistic to your interests and want a ticket to making trouble.

You can raise the entry fee for these nuisances by placing a minimum on the number of shares anyone must buy. A maximum on the number of shares can diminish the harm a speculator could do. But part of the cost of opening the door to public shareownership money is tolerating some of these less desirable family members.

Keeping your ideal in mind, the process turns to what is possible, given the investment proposition, schedule, and budget. Among those who can afford to invest, the following questions are what's relevant: Which ones are likely to become shareowners? How much will it cost to make them aware? How long and how much will it take to convert their awareness into a completed sale?

Answers to these questions will mostly be, "That depends." Depends on how effective the communications are, how good the media selection, how many prospects are converted to buyers. Targeting markets does not come first, all by itself. It is a back-and-forth process, with compromises and fine tuning, until the elements fit.

Media Selection

The way the message will be communicated to the target markets is very much affected by the schedule and budget. Your advertising agency and marketing consultant will be advising you on media selection. You can also do your own homework. Discover what others have to sell that most resembles your corporate shares, and what other businesses are likely to be marketing to the same target markets. Their products could be other financial products, like life insurance and mutual funds. But they may also be Jaguars and first-class resorts—or adult education courses and exercise programs. If the car dealer, college, and health club keep using the same media, it may mean that it has been successful for them. However, they may not necessarily be able to measure that. You could find it useful to have a telephone conversation with someone who appears to be marketing well to your identified groups.

Your advertising agency will have recommendations, backed by experiences and maybe even statistics. If those run against your feelings and your amateur research, keep the discussion alive for a while. No one knows your investment proposition as well as you do, and no one else will have to live with the new shareowners as you will.

There is really no limit to the media you may use, except cost-effectiveness and good taste. Direct share marketing programs have used a large variety of approaches (see Table 5.3). Market research continues throughout the marketing program design process. Interviews, focus groups, and literature searches will be feeding the team information about what has worked for others and what your target markets think and feel and believe. You can adjust your media mix as you go along, especially if you have a savvy media buyer on board.

Table 5.3. Advertising Approaches

Billboards	Direct mail	Point-of-sale posters
Broadcast TV	Endorsements	Public relations
Brochures	Magazine ads	Radio spots
Cable TV	Newspaper photo ads	Seminars

Test Marketing

You will also be test marketing to help you fine tune the program as it goes along. But here there is a big difference from marketing other products—because the only medium that can actually offer your shares is the prospectus. Your prospectus cannot be sent to prospective investors until it has cleared the SEC and any state reviews. Once the prospectus is cleared, it can only be used for a specific time before its information becomes stale and has to be updated. So there is not much time to test market with the actual share offering. Instead, the test marketing is done with the offer of a prospectus. All of the media is directed toward stimulating a request for a prospectus. Each message will be very clear that it is not offering shares—that they can only be offered by the prospectus.

Once your securities lawyer has filed with the SEC, you should get an estimate of when the prospectus can be cleared for sending to prospective investors. That is likely to be at least six weeks. So you have the time to test responses to the offer of a prospectus, and to make changes as a result of the tests. Your direct marketing specialist knows what size test is needed to make decisions.

This highlights a major difference between direct marketing and an underwriting. Securities brokers make a flurry of telephone calls to their customers and prospects, gathering "indications of interest" for shares. When the confirmations of sale are mailed, the prospectus accompanies it. So the sale actually takes place before the investor sees the prospectus. (The investor has five days to refuse to buy, to "renege.")

In direct marketing, the first objective is simply to generate a request for a prospectus. Then you fulfill that request by sending a prospectus, together with a stock order form. But the only thing your media program is "selling" is delivery of a prospectus, without any obligation to buy shares.

Your schedule and budget will be changed as a result of test marketing, as well as the continuing market research and flow of new ideas from the team. Media commitments will be beefed up or cut back. Copy and graphics may be revised. Follow-up efforts may be lessened or intensified. Some media bookings have lead times that prevent last-minute changes, but your agency can help you work around that.

ALLIES IN THE CAMPAIGN

There is only so much you can do in direct communication with your target groups. Your messages are about your corporation, its past, present, and future. Who will tell your prospects about what it is like to be a shareowner? Share-ownership will be a new adventure for many of them. It involves adding to the image of who they are—an addition they need to visualize before giving it a try. Many individuals in your target markets will need to become comfortable with seeing themselves as shareowners before they can consider the merits of your particular corporation.

There is very limited time and money for accomplishing these changes in self-perception and then completing a sale of your shares. You need all the allies you can get. These allies are people who are perceived by your market as independent experts on the subject of investing. They can include the local banker, minister, barber, accountant, and lawyer. Two groups worth special attention are securities brokers and financial planners.

Securities Brokers

Even if you do not pay them commissions, securities brokers may be a big help to you. They want to be known for recommending winners. Suggesting your shares to their friends and customers can create that image and build goodwill for them. Even if brokers do not recommend your shares, it will surely help if they do not discourage anyone who asks about your offering. What could be more natural for someone considering a share offering than to ask the opinion of a stockbroker?

Most of us react negatively when asked about an unknown, especially if we are supposed to be experts on the subject. How good could it be if we have not heard about it? Brokers need to be able to respond with, "Sure, I've talked with their president and read the prospectus."

One corporation marketed all of its first offering to people in the communities where it did business. On the eve of the offering, it had a cocktail party at the country club for all securities brokers in the area. Everyone there got a copy of the mailing that was about to go out and the newspaper ads that would soon appear. Reasons for using a direct offering were explained. Brokers were encouraged to ask questions and assured of access to corporate officers in the future. As a result, brokers were at least neutral when asked about the offering. Many actively encouraged their customers to buy a few shares from the corporation.

You will want to identify the brokers most likely to be consulted by your prospective shareowners. Then plan an information program just for them. Your securities lawyer may let you use a preliminary prospectus for this purpose. Even if the brokers are lukewarm, they will appreciate the advance knowledge of your offering.

Financial Planners

The term "financial planner" does not convey any clear picture in today's lineup of finance and investment professionals. Securities firms or life insurance companies use "financial planners" as a title for their brokers. Others who call themselves financial planners may really sell real estate syndications or other single-product investments.

There are "fee-only" financial planners, who are compensated only by their clients. They are far fewer in number than the financial planners who make most of their income from commissions on products they sell to their clients. Accountants and tax return preparers may double as financial planners, whether or not they use the title. Part of your market research and planning will be to come up with a useful list of people who really serve the function of financial planners.

Your list of financial planners will include the ones who might be consulted by individuals in your target markets. Your marketing program can then include a way to reach them and get their participation. This financial-planners component can include a campaign to educate people who are regularly asked for recommendations. They will include accountants, bankers, some lawyers, real estate brokers, and others who are expected to know about investing in corporate shares.

Other advisers will become apparent from your particular investment proposition. If you manufacture a health-care product, you can expect prospective investors to ask opinions from members of the professional group who would use your product. If it is software for managing construction, you will need to distribute shareownership marketing information to architects and contractors, especially those you know have a good opinion of your product.

Your basic goal is to get the shares sold within the brief time available. But you should also plan a continuous program for informing the people who will influence opinions about your corporation. They can generate fresh demand in the trading market for your shares. Keeping them informed will make your next offering much easier to sell.

Direct marketing of shareownership is like an election campaign. You go with what will win this time. But you must immediately start work to keep the interest up and build a base for the next offering.

YOUR INVESTMENT PROPOSAL

Remember the ten-word description of your business? Your marketing themes will be variations on that. Each target group may need a different approach, based on their particular dreams and desires. But they all need to be told the truth, as clearly and persuasively as will fit within their own frame of reference.

Your proposal is much more subtle than the usual appeals to basic needs. Selling food, clothing, or transportation only requires differentiating a product from the competition. Most of us are going to own a car, so why this one instead of another, and so forth. Messages tend to be about quality, value, extra benefits. Your message must go well beyond explaining why your corporation's shares are better than another's. You have to convince your market to invest in shares instead of doing something else with that money.

That is where your team becomes involved in the subtleties of motivators. There will be a continuous interplay among your profile of the perfect shareowners, your feel for groups with an affinity for your corporate shares, and the results from market research and test marketing.

Shareownership is a way to buy dreams—ones like your dentist's desire to be an entrepreneur, an employee's wanting to feel a part of the business, a young executive's ambition to "retire" early and pursue an art or a cause. Your marketing message can show the relationship between the dreams of your target markets and the realities of shareownership in your corporation.

Themes you develop for your initial share offering may set the tone for years to come. Be sure these themes feel comfortable, because changing the corporate image is both difficult and dangerous.

THE PROSPECTUS

Advertising, public relations, and direct marketing campaigns can only offer to send a prospectus and related marketing materials. Before it is furnished, the prospectus must have been filed and become effective with the SEC and state securities administrators. The Securities Act of 1933 declared that securities could only be offered to the public through a prospectus. Rules of the SEC describe what must be in a prospectus. This structure protects investors—if they ever read the prospectus before they invest. More often, it has protected the people selling securities. They cannot be liable for investor losses if they followed the rules— furnished a full and truthful prospectus and made no representations that were not also in the prospectus.

Most corporate shares have been sold by telephone calls from brokers. A prospectus has then been sent with the purchase confirmation and invoice. An investor has an opportunity to read it and back out of the purchase. Because of this procedure, the prospectus has been viewed as a "liability document." Despite encouragement by the SEC to make prospectuses more readable, they are generally very cold, imposing legal documents.

In direct marketing, your prospectus will be the principal source of persuasion, as well as the way you meet legal standards of information disclosure. You will actually be doing what was intended in the securities laws.

When you selected your securities lawyer, one of the objectives was to find one who could understand and endorse this use of a prospectus for its original purpose. You may have been fortunate enough to sign on a lawyer who can also write in a style that will be effective with your target markets. If not, there will have to be a collaboration between your securities lawyer and another member of the team.

SEC regulations actually encourage preparation of a prospectus that is useful in marketing. It can have an inviting appearance, with graphic and pictorial communication. There are rules showing how you may present forward-looking information, so you can tell where you plan to take the corporation, without making any promises and without disclosing any competitive secrets. Shares sell because of their prospects for the future. The basic rules are (1) follow the SEC's detailed guides for preparation, (2) tell the truth and the whole truth, and (3) keep it in good taste.

This third rule, good taste, can save a lot of grief, as well as time and expense. SEC staff attorneys and accountants who review prospectuses will be expecting something that looks like all the drab, dull ones they have seen before.

Be gentle with their sensibilities. If they are shocked or offended, it will be easy for them to pick your filing to pieces.

If you have a prospectus that is pleasing and interesting, as well as in legal compliance, you are less likely to have problems because you are different. You may even get some help from the SEC staff, especially if your lawyer has prepared them to be accepting and comfortable with your filing.

FULFILLING RESPONSES

All you expect to accomplish with advertising, public relations, and other channels is to receive requests for a prospectus, and the prospectus is all you can offer. In direct marketing terms, (1) your proposition is to give people a prospectus, (2) their response is to ask for one, (3) your fulfillment is to see that they get the prospectus. This process generates (4) a prospect for conversion into a shareowner in your company. Your team may feel the art and the fun is in the first and last steps, the proposition and the conversion. But all can quickly be lost in the middle two steps—getting the response and fulfilling it.

Mechanics for response and fulfillment must be clear and they must be quick. If you use a telephone response system, your responsibility schedule must accommodate having all the information ready before any proposition messages are ever prepared. Testing procedures need to be in place to make sure the system is working right. Response and fulfillment is where your information manager can shine. Speed is important. So is having useful information about the prospective shareowner, readily available for follow-up. If your project manager is not a detail person, you especially need a strong information systems manager. It might even be necessary to divide management along functional lines and have both managers report to you.

That is not to make light of the creative role in the response and fulfillment process. Increasing the response rate is perhaps the most useful of efforts. That often means new ideas for overcoming fear and inertia. The fulfillment package should renew the prospect's interest and lead to sending in an order, with payment, before any follow-up is necessary.

Closing the Sale

Conversion of leads into sales is often the forgotten step. It is not the most fun—only the most important. The following four basic closing options are available to you:

Hands Off. Fulfill telephone or mail responses by sending prospectuses and waiting for the order forms to be delivered;

In-House. Train some corporate employees to do limited telephone follow-up, without any "selling";

Hired Closers. Arrange for a registered broker-dealer to supervise a group of registered representatives; or

Broker-Assisted. Pay commissions for the sales closed by registered representantives of securities broker-dealers.

You are certainly not limited to choosing only one of these methods. At the outset, your marketing program was divided into segments, based on each target market's ability and likelihood to invest in your corporation's shares. Nowhere is that segmentation more useful than in planning the methods for closing sales.

Say you have five tiers of prospective investors, starting with 500 people who might buy $100,000 worth of shares and going down to level five, where the average investment is expected to be $3,000, and you have 80,000 prospects. Your closing efforts are going to be very different from the first level to the fifth. The specifics will depend on what your securities lawyer will sanction, on the schedule and budget, and on the people you have available for the project.

Those at the top level of your market pyramid, those who are likely to invest $100,000 or more, deserve personal meetings with you and other top officers. Not that they will get any information that is not available to everyone who reads the prospectus. Just that they are likely to expect the extra attention, and the results are worth the effort.

Prospective shareowners in the middle levels can be handled through in-house follow-up. This cannot be selling. It should be clerical, that is, just reminding the person who responded to complete their review of the prospectus and answering any mechanical questions about how to complete and return the order form. A telephone call to be sure the prospectus was received and to see if there are any questions. Directing those questions to places in the prospectus where they are answered. Reminding them of the closing date for orders.

This in-house follow-up is very serious business. Your training director will spend the most time with employees you ask to do this job. Supervision must be careful and consistent. Your securities lawyer needs to pass on the written instructions and the actual operation. At the bottom of the pyramid are responses to advertising in media chosen to reach people with an affinity for your company's product, location, or some other characteristic. Here you could use hired closers, or turn their information over to commissioned brokerage firms.

Choice of follow-up method for each group in your market pyramid depends on the results you are getting at the other levels. Not only the number of shares that have been sold, but also how closely the buyers resemble your profile of the ideal shareowner mix.

Hands Off

Billions of dollars of financial products are sold by mail and by telephone operators who only take orders. Insurance, mutual funds, and credit cards are all marketed, from initial communication to completed transaction, without any voices talking to each other at all.

The entire discount securities brokerage industry is founded on registered representatives who get paid a salary for executing orders. They do not give investment advice, whether requested or not. Nor do they initiate calls to solicit business. We have grown accustomed to parting with large amounts of money without having to see the building where it is going or developing a trust relationship with a real person.

There is an immense amount of experience with this type of closing. There are experts and wizards and gurus and mavens to be found. Formulas have been developed. Tiny details have been proven to increase response rates and conversion ratios, with precise cost/benefit analyses. Be sure you have one of these people on your team, at least for a half-day consulting session.

If all goes well, you will be selling more shares next year, or sooner. Part of your work is to build an information base about prospective investors. Not only who and where they are, but what works to get a response and a sale. Marketing shareownership should be a permanent part of your corporation's business. Hands-off closing is by far the cheapest and cleanest way to do it. It pays to keep getting better at it.

In-House

If your corporation has employees who are already dealing with people like your shareowner target groups, you may choose to organize your own telephone operation. It will be a major project in training and supervision. But, especially if you expect to have a series of share offerings, it can be the most effective way to meet your goals for financing and shareowner mix. If you use an in-house follow-up effort, your securities lawyer will be a major participant in the planning, training, and supervision.

The SEC has a "safe harbor" rule that protects employees who participate in selling their employer's shares, if they meet these simple standards: They have not been associated with a securities broker-dealer or sold securities in the preceding year, they have not been disqualified from the securities business, and they are not being compensated on the basis of shares sold. You will also have a training and supervision program for compliance with securities laws and your own rules.

There are so many positive results from an in-house closing program that it is worth pushing to get one going. For instance, the ability to discourage inappropriate shareowners. Some people should not be investing at the level of risk that your shares represent. Others may have completely wrong perceptions of what corporate shares are likely to bring them. If these people are not screened out at the offering, they will probably become unhappy shareowners later.

Another benefit from a thorough in-house closing component is the control you have over what is said about the shares, the corporation, and its management. We all read about the "boiler room" operations, in which securities are sold through high-pressure tactics. They take advantage of people's ignorance and greed. If the only ones talking to prospective investors about your offering are people you employ and supervise, there are fewer opportunities for misrepresentation. When someone buys shares, it should be for the right reason. This way, your corporation's reputation will not have to pay for some unauthorized sales pitch.

Your training program for in-house closers serves two purposes—the same two as your prospectus. It can develop successful techniques, and it can protect against violations of the securities laws and your own standards. One shareowner marketing consultant uses videos to simulate the conversations that are likely to occur. Written tests are administered, a manual is prepared for supervisors, and all of these materials become part of a record to show legal compliance. One of the ways you can protect against the mistakes of ambition and greed is to separate results of the closing operation from the compensation of its participants. No commissions. No bonuses based on the number of shares ordered.

Employees involved in the in-house closing effort will surely have their performance evaluated. Your project manager, securities lawyer, and employee trainer will have prepared an evaluation method. Before people get started, this method will be explained to them. It will deal with how well they screened prospective shareowners, how carefully they referred to the prospectus, and how diplomatically they refused to give any advice. Your securities lawyer can make or break an in-house closing program. If you see yourself using this method, discuss the subject when you interview securities lawyer candidates.

Hired Closers

There are people available who have licenses as a principal, a broker-dealer. They probably have considerable experience supervising registered representatives. Both the principals and the representatives can likely be found "between positions," especially with hard times in the brokerage and tax shelter businesses. There is no path cleared on this closing alternative. It seems like a logical approach, but you may want to wait until someone else has set a precedent.

Broker Assisted

Securities brokers can be a great help to you. You will need them to make a market in your stock, after the offering is over. That arrangement should be in place before you file with the SEC and state securities authorities. One of the most important bits of information for investors is how they can sell their shares when the time comes.

Brokers who make a trading market in your stock will be far better prepared, and probably more motivated, if they have also been involved in the offering itself. Just how they are involved is the challenge.

In a firm commitment underwriting, a securities firm does the selling exclusively, and the shares either get sold or the offering is cancelled. There is also a "best efforts" underwriting, in which the brokers sell as many of the shares as they can. Usually, that involves a minimum number that must be sold, and some best efforts offerings are done on an "all or nothing" basis. In either a firm commitment or best efforts underwriting, the securities brokerage firm generally uses telephone selling as the only marketing method. When you have a broker-assisted closing component in your direct share marketing, you still use all of the marketing media to generate interest and responses.

There are two basic ways to use brokerage firms when you are running your own share marketing program. You can select the firms and let them sell shares to their own customers and prospects. They will have the benefit of the advertising and public relations that you do, and you can furnish them sets of materials to give out. But they use their own relationships and prospect lists to generate sales.

The other way to use securities firms is to supply them with information gathered through responses to your marketing program. People in your target markets will be asked to call a telephone number, mail a coupon, or otherwise request an offering package that includes a prospectus. After they have received the written materials, a follow-up is in order. At this point you could turn the job over to your selected brokers.

Two Different Methods.   These two methods are very different. In the first, you are getting the brokers, their relationships with customers, and the fruits of their own prospecting efforts. There could be some overlap with your own targeted markets, but you would be making no attempt to coordinate the brokers' selling efforts with your own follow-up procedures. In the second method, the brokerage firm's registered representatives become an arm of your marketing program.

You are subcontracting the closing step to them. They are not required to trade on their existing relationships. In fact, you are helping them get to know people who have expressed interest in buying corporate shares, one of the products the brokers sell. (Your lawyer will have to prepare an agreement that protects you from having your leads switched to other brokerage products.)

You will want to think about the implications of your use of brokers, and discuss them with your team, directors, and other advisors. Some of the questions that will come up, after you have decided to use a broker-assisted closing for some of your shares are: Should your marketing materials tell people that a securities broker may call them to help with their decision? Should your materials list brokers for your target markets to call with any questions? If you do this, should you also give information to the brokers from responses received in-house? Should you use broker follow-up for responses from people in the lowest probability level of market groups, while using in-house follow-up for the better prospects? Should you only bring in the brokers if you have not sold some minimum number of shares by a certain date in your program?

A Different Option.   A different option is simply to meet with brokers and keep them informed, but not include them in your marketing program at all. Your purpose is to get their good will and future cooperation in market making. This has worked nicely where the brokers understood the reasons for a direct offering and did not feel at all threatened by it. Not only did they stay away from saying discouraging things about the offering, many of them actually recommended that their customers buy shares directly.

One of the big advantages that direct marketing offers is the relationship built with shareowners, and among financial advisors and the business news reporters. It may not be wise to bring a broker in between you and these supporters. You "own" this relationship. It can become a valuable corporate asset. There may be many fears about using brokers. But the fact is that you need to close sales for all the shares within a fairly short time. Brokers are in that business. Unless you are confident you can sell without them, it is just a matter of how you define and control their participation.

Should you fear that marketing shares directly to investors may cause retaliation by securities brokers, because you cut their commissions and poached on their franchise to sell securities? You can imagine them refusing to trade in "tainted shares," as if they had been sold in some gray market. Brokers could boycott any future securities offerings by your corporation. Those fears have proved ground-less. In direct offerings so far, the opportunity to make the trading market has appealed to brokerage firms, whether the shares had been underwritten or marketed directly. If a corporation has a profitable transaction to do, its history of direct marketing has not discouraged anybody.

Broker's Commissions.   Brokers are accustomed to working entirely on commission. They are given a product to sell and told how much they will get paid for each unit sold. It is not likely to be worthwhile dreaming up some other plan for paying them. There is enough new in your share marketing program without confusing the compensation package. What ends up in the broker's paycheck is the product of two factors—the commission your corporation pays and how that commission is split between the individual broker and the securities firm.

Do *not* try to pay the broker directly. Any commissions must go through the firm, to be split according to their policy. You can discuss both the commission and the broker's payout with the firm's executives. Maybe they will agree to a more generous percentage for the broker. You can argue that you are providing the marketing support (and, if you choose, follow-up prospect lists). You are also handling some of the paperwork that the firm's back office would usually get. Another argument is that the firm stands to get future business from market making and your corporation's future financings.

There are some comparative levels you can use when setting a commission rate for brokers selling to their own customers and prospects they generate. For instance, (1) the selling broker's firm gets about 4.5% in a firm commitment initial public offering managed by a Wall Street investment banker. (2) Selling a corporate share mutual fund could mean from 3 to 8.5%, depending on the order size and whether the fund is "full load" or "low load." (3) Real estate limited partnerships often carry 9% commissions, but they take more time to explain. And (4) insured certificates of deposit pay no more than 2%, but brokers hope to capture money from new customers, and then sell higher commission securities when the CDs mature. Whatever commission and payout structure you agree on with one firm, try to use the same one with every other set of brokers. Although the industry is fiercely competitive, word does get around, and no one likes to be treated less well than a peer.

The securities industry will continue to experience immense changes. Out of these will come opportunities for having registered sales people market shareownership without an underwriting. Corporations will be able to creatively match their own needs with those of the individual brokers and their securities firm employers.

AFTER THE OFFERING IS OVER

You are now a public company. Your corporation has a stature and an access to money that enables you to perform in any league. The price is a continuing responsibility to shareowners and their representatives in government, in the news media, and in such investor service roles as brokers, financial planners, and newsletter publishers.

Securities Law Compliance

Your securities lawyer should give you a memorandum about the filings you will make and the way you need to handle such matters as news releases and insider stock trades. Make someone on your staff the compliance officer, perhaps your personal assistant. Have this person learn from reading and talking to counterparts. Many people are quoted as saying that compliance costs $100,000 a year. That is several times more than necessary. Just keep the job away from your lawyers and accountants as much as possible.

Shareowner Relations

Marketing shareownership is an ongoing part of the business for a public corporation. You will want to treat shareownership just as you would one of your major product lines. The manager in charge of shareownership reports to you, with a plan and a budget.

There are independent shareowner relations consultants who can get you started and guide your assigned shareowner relations manager. One direct share marketing consultant furnishes a written program, training, and on-going advice. You have several good reasons—maintaining a fair price, preparing for the next offering, discouraging raiders and strikers, nurturing ambassadors of good will—for working on your relationship directly with those share-owners.

Maintaining a Fair Price. There are many different ways to calculate what corporate shares are worth. Most of those ways involve predicting the future, based on the recent past. Problems come up when shareowners feel they are uninformed, or that a select few have better information than they do. If you keep everyone informed of what is happening and what you expect to happen, your share price will probably remain fair to everyone. Sharing information promptly and accurately also prevents recurrent waves of buying and selling. As a result, you can have a market price that moves rather slowly in relation to the stock market averages—a low beta stock. That will make shareowners more comfortable and discourage speculators.

Preparing for the Next Offering. Many corporate managers feel they can only have share offerings when their investment bankers tell them the market is receptive. Unfortunately, the market goes in cycles that often have no relationship to the corporation's need for capital. One of the objectives for direct marketing of shareownership is to be free of cycles for underwritten offerings and largely independent of stock market trends. Your continuous marketing program should build a loyal base of shareowners who will want to buy more in the next offering. You can also create interest in individuals and their advisers who do not yet own your shares, so there is some overhanging demand for the next offering.

Discouraging Raiders and Strikers. One of the big negatives mentioned in going public is the possibility of attracting a corporate raider. These are the predators who take advantage of underpriced shares to make a quick profit. Raiders often buy control of a corporation and then sell it in pieces. If the founders and management still own a majority of the shares, this is not a worry. But a raider could still demand a seat on the board and otherwise become a nuisance, perhaps with the objective of collecting "greenmail" by selling the shares back to the corporation at a profit.

For a raider to be interested, your shares must be below a fair price. However else a price is calculated, if it has fallen below the corporation's liquidation value, something is seriously wrong. Part of it is often a lack of attention to keeping shareowners informed about what management is trying to do.

The other big source of trouble is the person who owns a few shares and sues, claiming some fraud on the market by management. The term "strike suit" is used when the objective seems to be getting management to settle quickly, in order to get rid of the case. Often this litigation strikes just when it would most interfere with the corporation's plans. Whatever the merits of the claimed wrongs, there can be no lawsuit if there are no damages. Strike suits occur when shares have been purchased at a considerably higher price than what the market quotes when the case is filed. In a stable market, the price change will not be worth starting the fight.

Nurturing Ambassadors of Good Will. Shareowners can do much more for the corporation than provide capital and support a fair market price. They can help themselves by helping the corporation, beyond just buying your products.

When you imagined your ideal shareowner mix, you probably included customers, suppliers, employees, and members of the corporation's local community. Keeping those people well informed can encourage them to support your position in other areas as well.

Political issues will often be important to your business, whether at a local planning agency or a congressional subcommittee. Shareholders may be better at presenting your case than you could alone. Support from shareowners can translate into finding key employees, uncovering possible acquisitions, and just getting some refreshing outside management advice. These bonuses will come from shareowners who feel they are a part of the corporation, not just a source of money.

CONCLUSION

Entrepreneuers and managers will sell shares in their corporations because they believe it is the best way to get money for those businesses. Individuals will buy those shares because they believe it is the best way to achieve some of their own personal objectives. Direct marketing is simply the most effective way for these individual objectives to accommodate each other.

As the channel for matching businesses and shareowners is opened through direct marketing, there can be some pronounced effects on the way corporations are structured and how they affect society as a whole.

SCOR—For Offerings Under $1 Million

A long political pilgrimage is finally leading to some real help in matching entrepreneurs and individual investors. Public offerings for up to $1 million can now be made without a registration statement filed with the SEC. Cost savings of as much as $100,000 have been estimated by entrepreneurs who have used the process.

Congress enacted the Small Business Investment Incentive Act of 1980, calling for federal and state cooperation to diminish the burden for small businesses trying to raise capital. Two years later, the SEC adopted its Rule 504, exempting small public offerings from federal registration if they follow state requirements, including a disclosure document for investors.

Then a subcommittee of the American Bar Association spent three years coming up with a uniform filing and disclosure form that the states could use. The State Regulation of Securities Committee, through the Subcommittee on Private Offering Exemption and Simplification of Capital Formation, appointed the Rule 504 study group of four lawyers. They are Jean E. Harris, O'Connor, Cavanagh, Anderson, Westover, Killingsworth & Beshears (Phoenix); Stanley Keller, Palmer & Dodge (Boston); G. Michael Stakias Blank, Rome, Comisky & McCauley (Philadelphia), and Mike Liles, Jr. of Bogle & Gates (Seattle).

They reported their progress through three articles in *The Business Lawyer*, Vol. 43 page 757, Vol. 44 page 625, and Vol. 45 page 1343. In contrast to the ever longer and more complex SEC prospectuses, the lawyer group has said they sought "readability by persons who are not financial professionals" (43, *The Business Lawyer* p. 761).

In April 1989, the proposed form was approved by the North American Securities Administrators Association (NASAA), which named it the Small Corporate Offering Registration (SCOR). NASAA added SCOR as Form U-7 to its uniform state securities filings. A very short and simple filing has to be made with the SEC, *after* an offering is sold. Frequent progress reports are filed with the states during a selling period that can take up to a year.

Several state legislatures quickly adopted the necessary securities laws, which have included relaxation of some of their own requirements. (Some have used the acronym "ULOR," Uniform Limited Offering Registration.) In 1989, the SEC raised the original $500,000 maximum to $1 million, provided that at least half the amount is sold under the SCOR procedure.

The features and savings available under SCOR are described in each State's instructions. They follow the Small Corporate Offering Registration Form, as adopted by NASAA on April 29, 1989, from which the following summary has been drawn:

> **Marketing**. A "firm commitment" underwriting is not permitted (that is, one where securities firms commit to buy and instantly resell the shares). Sales are made through direct marketing or by using commissioned securities agents. Telephone and in-person marketing is permitted (participants may have to be registered under state law). No limit is placed on the number or status of the persons to whom the offering is made.

Documents. There has been a real effort to make the "disclosure document" serve as the marketing tool. Any ads or other written materials must be cleared by the state regulators and limited to brief announcements and instructions for getting a disclosure document.

Lawyers. Legal compliance can be accomplished by most small business attorneys without hiring a special securities lawyer. The only legal opinion required is one that states that the shares have been duly authorized and will be legally and validly issued, fully paid and nonassessable and binding on the company. Offerings have been done with legal fees of about $10,000.

Auditors. Audited financial statements are not required for the first $500,000 of securities offered by a company. The accounting profession has announced it will follow this procedure and permit "reviewed" financials, in accordance with accounting standards. Even when an audit is made, there is no "comfort letter" requirement, and very little extra cost for auditors should be necessary. Auditors fees for SCOR offerings have often been in the $10,000 to $15,000 range.

Printing. Because there is no firm commitment underwriting, special financial printers need not be used. The disclosure document can be taken to desktop composition or camera-ready form on a word processor. It should be many pages shorter than an SEC prospectus.

Filings. Since SCOR is a uniform filing, the same documents can be used in any state that has passed appropriate legislation. The instructions are short and in plain English. Completing the form is a process of answering questions (which some states will provide on computer disk). The resulting disclosure document will include a business plan and a listing of the principal risks to investors. Filing fees in some states are about $500.

In addition to making small public offerings easier, some states are actively promoting the offerings. Washington state compiled its own mailing list of prospective investors, by sending questionnaires to a list it developed of people who would probably have the ability to and interest in buying the shares. Companies can have an announcement sent by the state to those on this list, telling people where they can request that firm's disclosure document. Washington has publicized the availability of the process and published a booklet, "A Consumers Guide to Making Venture Investments in Small Business."

After Arizona's legislature unanimously adopted SCOR in May 1990, a special assistant to the securities division director was hired to help the program become active. By the end of 1990, 18 states had adopted the SCOR legislation. Qualifying in any SCOR state also allows sales to be made in New York, Colorado, and the District of Columbia. The status of SCOR in any jurisdiction can be determined by a call to the state securities regulator.

More information about SCOR may be available from any state's securities regulator. Here are names of people who have expressed a willingness to provide information:

Washington: Greg Toms, Securities Analyst
Manager of Small Business Section
Securities Division, Department of
Licensing
P.O. Box 648, Olympia, WA 98504
(206) 753-6928

Ronald E. Schutz, Investment Specialist
Washington State Business Assistance
Center
2001 6th Avenue, Suite 2700
Seattle, WA 98121
(206) 464-6282, ext. 307

Arizona: Sandra J. Forbes, Assistant to the
Director of Securities for Law and Policy
Arizona Corporation Commission,
Securities Division
1200 West Washington
Phoenix, AZ 85007
(602) 542-0622

Progress of SCOR is being monitored by the SEC, which is considering related moves to help improve capital formation for smaller businesses. The SEC person responsible is Mary Beach, Associate Director of Small Business, Division of Corporation Finance, Washington, DC, 20549, (202) 272-2585.

Bibliography

This listing of books is divided into several categories. Each group is arranged by year of publication, with the most recent one first. The commentaries in parentheses are the author's view of how useful the books are for their intended purpose.

Books for entrepreneurs on going public:

Weiss, M. *Going Public: How to Make Your Initial Public Offering Successful.* Blue Ridge Summit: Liberty House, 1988.

    Ninety pages of advice about an underwritten public offering by a retired chief financial officer of a company which had gone public. The rest of the book is a copy of the prospectus used in an underwritten offering—like those available free from securities brokers.

Sutton, D. P. and Benedetto, M. W. *Initial Public Offerings: A Strategic Planner for Raising Capital.* Chicago: Probus, 1988. Reissued in paperback in 1990 with the subtitle: *All You Need to Know About Taking a Company Public.*

  Written by a former investment banker and a financial writer, this book deals exclusively with firm commitment underwritings. Half the book consists of a reprinted prospectus and other public documents.

Each of the following books is currently out of print and available only in some libraries and used book stores. They are also limited to underwritten public offerings.

O'Flaherty, J. S. *Going Public: The Entrepreneur's Guide.* New York: John Wiley & Sons, 1984.

Berman, D. S. *Going Public: A Practical Handbook of Procedures and Forms.* Englewood Cliffs: Prentice-Hall, 1974.

  This has a brief section (pages 29-31) on "Do It Yourself" stock sales, limited to informal financing with a list of friends and suppliers.

Weaver, Jr., R. A. *Initial Public Financing for the Small & Medium Sized Business.* New York: Investment Bankers Association of America (now the Securities Industry Association), 1969.

Winter, E. L. *A Complete Guide to Making a Public Stock Offering.* Englewood Cliffs: Prentice-Hall, 1962.

  This book is still useful as a guide for an underwritten initial public offering. It could be particularly helpful to an entrepreneur, since it was written by the president of a company that successfully completed the process.

Information about the following books was obtained from the National Union Catalog, published by the Library of Congress. I have not been able to find them.

Lewis, S. H. *Taking a Private Company Public.* Published by its author, 1984.

Roberts, E. W. *How, When and Where to Go Public with a Small Company.* New York: Exposition Press, 1973.

Hutchison, G. S. *Why, When, and How to Go Public.* New York: Presidents Publishing House, 1970.

There are many pamphlets available free from the large accounting and printing firms. Names for each are in the Glossary, under *Auditors* and *Financial printers*.

Books directed primarily to lawyers:

Mechanics of Underwriting 1991 and *1989.* New York: Practising Law Institute.

These are materials prepared by participants for educational programs. Some are just sparse outlines of little value for persons not attending the sessions. Others include useful forms and descriptions not otherwise publicly available.

Bloomenthal, H. S. *1990 Going Public Handbook.* New York: Clark Boardman Company, 1990.

This is much more than "handbook" would suggest. It has good explanations and useful forms, presented for lawyers not particularly experienced in securities matters.

Soderquist, L. D. *Understanding the Securities Laws.* New York: Practising Law Institute, 1990.

A basic guide for lawyers in general business practice or entrepreneurs who want a foundation in the legal process of going public and being publicly traded.

How to Prepare an Initial Public Offering 1989. New York: Practising Law Institute, 1989.

For a course handbook, this one has unusually clear and thorough detail on deciding to go public, selecting an underwriter, and the registration process.

Bloomenthal, H. S. *Going Public and the Public Corporation.* New York: Clark Boardman Company, 1987.

> By the same author and publisher as the *Going Public Handbook;* this is easier to read, but with fewer practical tools.

Halloran, M. J. *Public Offering Negotiation.* Englewood Cliffs: Prentice Hall Law & Business, 1986.

> For companies determined to go the underwritten public offering route, written by an experienced securities lawyer. This book is also helpful in deciding whether to use an underwriter at all.

Bialkin, K. J. and Grant, Jr., W. J., (eds.) *Securities Underwriting: A Practitioner's Guide,* New York: Practising Law Institute, 1985.

> This is an excellent source of information that is otherwise found only in the minds of securities lawyers.

Halloran, M. J. *Venture Capital and Public Offering Negotiation.* Englewood Cliffs: Prentice Hall Law and Business, 1982.

> This collection of papers is directed primarily to the company that goes through a few rounds of venture capital private placements and then is taken public through an underwriter. It is a very detailed reference work with annual supplements.

The following books are likely to be found only in law firm libraries or large used book stores. Their age makes them somewhat dangerous for anything other than general education or history.

Going Public in the 80's. New York: Law Journals Seminar-Press, 1982.

Frome, R. L. *Raising Capital.* Law & Business, 1981.

Hot New Issues—First Time Filings. New York: New York Law Journal, 1972.

Robinson, G. J. *Going Public: Successful Securities Underwriting.* New York: Clark Boardman, 1971.

Going Public Workshop—1970. New York: Practising Law Institute, 1970.

Going Public-Advanced Techniques. New York: Practising Law Institute, 1970.

The following two books are referenced in other sources, but I have not been able to find them.

Lubben, D. J., *Procedures and Problems in a Public Offering.* N. p., n. d.

The Anatomy of a Public Offering, N. p., 1978.

Books for Certified Public Accountants:

Levitin, M. S., *Helping Your Small Business Client Go Public.* New York: American Institute of CPAs, 1985.

Books for going public in Canada or England:

Several U. S. companies have chosen to have their initial public offerings occur in these other countries. More and more European and Asian countries are developing active stock markets, with a much higher proportion of individual participants. This may be a reasonable alternative, in countries where the company actually does business and has some name recognition.

Pogue, P. T. *Going Public on the Vancouver Stock Exchange.* Kansas City: International Newsmedia, 1987.

Byford, B. *Going Public on the Vancouver Stock Exchange.* Creative Corporate Financings Techniques, 1985.

The Vancouver Stock Exchange has had significant unfavorable publicity on occasion. It has also been about the

only chance for some companies to do an underwritten public offering.

Richardson, M. *Going Public*. London: Business Books, 1976.

McQuillan, P. E. *Going Public in Canada*. N.p., 1971.

General books which include public share offerings:

None of the more general business finance books call attention to the potential of direct share marketing, except for the first one on the list. The rest are useful in finding other sources of financing a business.

Lindsey, J. *The Entrepreneur's Guide to . . . Capital: Over 150 Proven Ways to Finance New & Growing Businesses*. Chicago: Probus, 1990.
      This is the one "how to raise capital" book in which more than a sentence or two was found about direct public offerings. Its Chapter 21, "Self-Underwriting," has some useful suggestions, particularly on preparing for the day when the company may go public.

Altman, R. M. *Creating Investor Demand for Company Stock*. Westport: Quorum Books, 1988.

Inc. Magazine, eds., Part III, "Equity Financing: Going Public." In *The Best of Inc. Guide to Finding Capital*. Englewood Cliffs: Prentice Hall Press, 1988.

Harrock, R. D., ed. "Planning the Business for a Future Initial Public Offering." In *Start-Up Companies: Planning, Financing, and Operating the Successful Business*. Law Journals Seminar-Press, 1988.

Dow Jones-Irwin. *Handbook for Raising Capital*. Homewood: Dow Jones-Irwin, 1987.

Owen, R. R. *The Arthur Young Guide to Financing for Growth: Ten Alternatives for Raising Capital*. New York: John Wiley & Sons, 1986.

Colman, R. *Modern Business Financing*. Englewood Cliffs: Prentice Hall, 1985.

Postyn, S. and Postyn, J. K. *Raising Cash*. Belmont: Lifetime Learning Publications/Wadsworth, 1982.
The authors have been through the start-up to public company experience as managers and as advisers from the inside and out.

Gordon, M. J. *The Investment, Financing and Valuation of the Corporation*. Westport: Greenwood Press, 1982 (reprint of the 1962 edition).

Diener, R. *How to Finance Your Growing Business*. Englewood Cliffs: Prentice Hall, 1981.
Particularly Chapter 12, "Public Stock Issues."

Wert, J. E. and Henderson, Jr. G. V. *Financing Business Firms*, Homewood: R. D. Irwin, 1979.

Auden, C., *How to Finance Your Company*. Woodstock: Beekman Publishers, 1977.

Books about maintaining investor interest in shares:

Mahoney, W. F. *Investor Relations: The Professional's Guide To Financial Marketing and Communications*. New York: New York Institute of Finance, 1991.

Marcus, B. W. *Competing for Capital: A Financial Relations Approach*. New York: John Wiley & Sons, 1975.
Though now dated, it lays a good foundation for the importance of bringing the responsibility for keeping interest in a company's shares in-house.

Roalman, A. R., ed. *Investor Relations Handbook*. Under the auspices of the National Investor Relations Institute, New York: AMACOM, 1974.
Some useful advice and case histories from experienced contributors.

Books about financial analysis:

These books are at varying levels of complexity, roughly in proportion to their price, which is shown for several of

them. They can be useful in at least two ways: (1) deciding whether a company is ready to go public and (2) understanding how investors may value a company.

Bernstein, L. J. R. *Analysis of Financial Statements*, 3d ed. Homewood: D. Irwin, 1990, $39.95.

Siegel, J. G. and Shim, J. K., *Thinking Finance.* New York: Harper Business, 1990, $17.95.

Bernstein, L. A. *Financial Statement Analysis: Theory, Application and Interpretation.* 4th ed. Homewood: R. D. Irwin, 1989, $52.00.

Harrington, D. R. and Wilson, B. D. *Corporate Financial Analysis.* Homewood: Dow Jones-Irwin, 1989, $29.95.

Ritchie, Jr., J. C. *Fundamental Analysis.* Chicago: Probus, 1989, $24.95.

Donnahoe, A. S. *What Every Manager Should Know About Financial Analysis.* New York: Simon & Schuster, 1989.

Cottle, S., Murray, R. F., and Block, F. E. *Graham and Dodd's Security Analysis,* 5th ed. New York: McGraw-Hill, 1988.
    This is an updated edition of the classic text for fundamental, or "value" investing.

Levine, S. N., ed. *The Financial Analysts Handbook,* 2d ed. Homewood: Dow Jones-Irwin, 1988, $80.00.

Woelfel, C. J. *Financial Statement Analysis.* Chicago: Probus, 1988, $21.95.

Helfert, E. A. *Techniques of Financial Analysis,* 6th ed. Homewood: R. D. Irwin, 1987, $27.50.

Downes, J. and Goodman, J. E., *Dictionary of Finance and Investment Terms.* Happauge: Barron's Educational Series, 1987, $9.95.

Finnerty, J. D. *Corporate Financial Analysis.* New York: McGraw-Hill, 1986, $57.95.

Droms, W. G. *Finance and Accounting for Nonfinancial Managers.* Reading: Addison-Wesley, 1983, $12.95.

Linneman, R. E. *Shirt-Sleeve Approach to Long-Range Planning for the Smaller, Growing Corporation.* Englewood Cliffs: Prentice Hall, 1980.

Books about the changes on Wall Street:

Lowenstein, L. *What's Wrong With Wall Street.* Reading: Addison-Wesley, 1988.

 Deals mostly with the trading and takeover markets. Its only recommendations are a couple of minor changes in the securities laws.

Hayes III, S. L.; Spence, A. M.; and Marks, D. V. P. *Competition in the Investment Banking Industry.* Cambridge: Harvard University Press, 1983.

 Statistics, graphs, and commentaries for an economic-policy view of Wall Street.

Goldberg, L. G. and White, L. J., ed.*The Deregulation of the Banking and Securities Industries.* Lexington: Lexington Books, 1979.

 A collection of rather scholarly essays on the legal and economic changes which have affected financial intermediaries in the last two decades.

Lechner, A. *Street Games: Inside Stories of the Wall Street Hustle.* New York: Harper & Row, 1980.

 Mostly anecdotes which colorfully illustrated the changes on Wall Street in the 1970s.

Twentieth Century Fund. *Abuse on Wall Street: Conflicts of Interest in the Securities Markets.* Westport: Greenwood Press, 1980.

 This is the report of several commissioned investigations. Two sections are excellent revelations of how the underwriting and trading market systems work: "Investment Banking" by Nicholas Wolfson and "Broker-Dealer Firms" by Martin Mayer.

Blume, M. E. and Friend, I. *The Changing Role of the Individual Investor.* (Twentieth Century Fund, sponsors.) New York: John Wiley & Sons, 1978.

    An academic study of the shift from a stock market for individuals to one dominated by institutional investors and their money managers.

Sobel, R. *Inside Wall Street: Continuity and Change in the Financial District.* New York: W. W. Norton, 1977.

    An easy-to-read history of the securities industry by the author of numerous books about corporations and the financial markets. The bibliography, pages 273–279, can lead to many hours of a reading for those who have become fascinated with the American financial markets.

Welles, C. *The Last Days of the Club.* New York: E. P. Dutton, 1975.

    The history of the New York Stock Exchange, told by one of our best financial writers. Reading it today illustrates how clear the trend has been on Wall Street for many years, but how slowly the changes evolve.

Carosso, V. P. *Investment Banking in America.* Cambridge: Harvard University Press, 1970.

    A magnificent history. It shows how direct marketing with a standby underwriter was replaced by investment bankers who actually carried the market risk and sponsored a company's shares; and how that was converted into an underwriting syndicate that put the risk back onto the company, but held onto the full markup.

Schwed, Jr., F. *Where Are the Customers' Yachts? . . . or a Good Hard Look at Wall Street.* New York: Simon and Schuster, 1955.

    This is the "Bull Market Edition," augmented by its author of a book first published in 1940. The truth in its humor explains what has happened since publication.

Books about direct marketing:

Any book on this subject will have something useful for planning and managing a direct public offering. These are suggested for a foundation.

David Shepard Associates, *The New Direct Marketing.* Homewood: Dow Jones-Irwin, 1990.

    The "new" direct marketing emphasizes database technology and statistical techniques for identifying and learning about prospects. The "old" direct marketing relied more on the attention-grabbing quality of the message and media.

Gross, M. *The Direct Marketer's Idea Book.* New York: AMACOM, 1989.

    A gathering of individual ideas for quick reference, including a short chapter on promoting financial services through direct marketing.

Retzler, K. *Direct Marketing: The Proven Path to Successful Sales.* Glenview: Scott, Foresman, 1988.

    A basic introduction with some helpful tools.

Nicholas, T. *The Golden Mailbox: Ted Nicholas on Direct Marketing.* Wilmington: Enterprise Publishing, 1988.

    Primarily about direct mail, by one of the old hands at the art.

Holtz, H. *The Direct Marketer's Workbook.* New York: John Wiley & Sons, 1986.

    Some useful procedures, checklists, and practical tips.

Godsen, Jr., F. F. *Direct Marketing Success.* New York: John Wiley & Sons, 1985.

    A beginner's book.

Kobs, J. *Profitable Direct Marketing.* Lincolnwood: NTC Business Books, 1979 (reprinted 1988).

    The case studies are particularly helpful.

Stone, B. *Successful Direct Marketing Methods.* Chicago: Crain Books, 1975.

On page 1, this guru defined direct marketing as "controlled messages to defined audiences, each message with a single purpose—to get a response."

Books on telemarketing:

Idelman, S. A. *How to Manage Growth and Maximize Profits in Outbound Telemarketing.* Englewood Cliffs: Prentice Hall, 1989.

A detailed program for a business based on telemarketing, but also useful if telemarketing will be a big part of a direct public offering.

Fidel, S. L. *Start-Up Telemarketing.* New York: John Wiley & Sons, 1987.

Good for the basics of telemarketing.

Books on marketing generally:

Among the many books on marketing, these are some that are helpful in doing a direct public offering.

Beitman, H. *Financial Services Marketing.* Blue Ridge Summit: TAB Books, 1990.

Much of the technique for marketing financial services can be carried over to marketing shareownership. This is a good primer.

Debelak, D. *Total Marketing: Capturing Customers with Marketing Plans that Work.* Homewood: Dow Jones-Irwin, 1989.

Good strategies for picking markets, developing marketing plans, and communicating messages.

Stanley, T. J. *Marketing to the Affluent.* Homewood: Dow Jones-Irwin, 1988.

How to identify, learn about, and communicate effectively with people who can afford to buy corporate shares.

Imber, J. and Toffler, B. *Dictionary of Advertising and Direct Mail Terms.* Happauge: Barron's Education Series, 1987.
> A handy reference.

Templeton, J. F. *Focus Groups: A Guide for Marketing and Advertising Professionals.* Chicago: Probus, 1987.
> More than you may ever need to know, but important if you are going to base a marketing plan on this form of market research.

Books on inexpensive marketing:

A direct share marketing program does not need the mass marketing used for general consumer products. These books are especially helpful in long-term methods of getting your company's story into the minds of prospective shareowners, without violating the securities laws.

Phillips, M. and Rasberry, S. *Marketing Without Advertising.* Berkeley: Nolo Press, 1986 (reprinted in 1990).
> Michael is a friend of mine, but the book would still be recommended for its long-term, word-of-mouth program to build interest in your company.

Slutsky, J. *Street Smart Marketing.* New York: John Wiley & Sons, 1989.
> Lots of alternatives to expensive advertising and direct marketing.

Weinrauch, J. D. and Craft Baker, N. *The Frugal Marketer.* New York: AMACOM, 1989.
> An alphabetically arranged commentary on marketing subjects. Skimming through the large number of topics could trigger interest in more serious study.

Davidson, J. P., *Marketing on a Shoestring.* New York: John Wiley & Sons, 1988.
> Information and ideas for cutting out waste.

Glossary

This glossary is offered as a reference for looking up the meaning of terms relating to corporate shares, public offerings, or direct marketing. Reading it is also another way to understand the book's basic message:

1. companies are not selling shares to the public because the underwriting syndicate no longer works,
2. there is plenty of money and motivation among individuals to invest as shareowners, and
3. here is how you can take your company public through direct marketing.

Like any speciality, corporate finance has its own argot seemingly designed to intimidate the outsider. Many everyday words take on new connotations when applied to public stock offerings. Then there are the terms created by lawyers, regulators, and practitioners of the relatively new direct marketing speciality. The meanings and commentary in this glossary are the author's own interpretations.

Note: Terms in italics are defined in their alphabetical order.

Acceleration Securities cannot be sold unless a *registration statement* has become effective with the *SEC*, or a specific exemption applies. That *effective date* occurs automatically 20 days after it is filed, unless an *SEC* stop order or refusal order is in effect. The way it really works is that each filing includes a *delaying amendment* so that it cannot become effective automatically. Then the lawyers file a request for acceleration of the effective date to a selected day and time.

Aftermarket The *trading market* that develops for *shares* after the *public offering* is over. Orders to buy or sell shares are matched in the *over-the-counter market* by a *securities firm* acting as a *market maker*. For *listed shares*, a *specialist* on the *stock exchange* will match orders. The quality of the aftermarket is measured by its ability to absorb *bid* or *asked* orders without major disruptions in the price. That ability is a function of the market's *liquidity*—the number of shares owned by the public, rather than by company *insiders* (called the *float*), and the extent to which the public is active in trading the shares, rather than holding them for the long term.

Agreement among underwriters In the last few weeks before the *effective date* of an *underwritten public offering*, the *managing underwriter* will be putting together an *underwriting syndicate* of other *securities firms*. When the *underwriting agreement* is signed, the firms who have joined will sign an agreement among underwriters, assigning them an *allotment* of shares they are technically required to buy from the company as an *underwriter*.

All hands meetings Part of the ritual for an *underwritten public offering* is the all hands meeting. These gatherings include an initial planning meeting (the "kickoff meeting") and at least two sessions for reviewing drafts of the *registration statement*. They include two or more representatives each from the company, the company's general counsel and its securities lawyers, the *managing underwriter*, the law firm representing the underwriters, and the *auditors*. The kickoff meeting may have people from the *financial printer*, *transfer agent*, and *registrar*. The meetings go on for at least a full day, often for two or three. The kickoff meeting is often consumed with a power struggle among representatives of the *investment bankers*, the company and their respective counsel to settle who will be the "quarterback" for the preparation process. Some drafting sessions will last through the night to meet a deadline set by the *time and responsibility schedule*.

All-or-none offering Each *public offering* will have a total number of *shares* to be sold. Sometimes, in a *direct public offering* or a *best efforts underwriting*, a condition of the offering will be that all shares offered must be sold or the offering is cancelled and none of the shares will be sold.

Allotment In an *underwritten public offering*, each *securities firm* in the *underwriting syndicate* is allocated an *allotment* of shares to sell. As a practical matter there is very little relationship between the allotment and actual sales. Technically, the *agreement among underwriters* could force each member of the *underwriting syndicate* to take its allotment.

Angel investors Also known as *informal investors*, these are people who invest money in the business at its start-up, or "seed capital" stage, before other sources of *capital* would be available. They are usually relatives or friends of the entrepreneur, or individuals with the wealth and experience to take significant risks for possible long-term rewards. Angel investors and entrepreneurs often get together through acquaintances or *finders*. The transaction is usually negotiated as a *private placement*. According to a survey made for the Small Business Administration, angel investors were the largest source of external equity capital for small businesses in the United States, at about $30 billion a year.

Annual report Financial statements and a *management's discussion and analysis* of the company's operations and condition. For companies with *registered shares* under the federal *Securities Exchange Act of 1934*, an annual report must be filed with the *SEC*, following Form 10-K. Most states require corporations to send annual reports to their *shareowners*. These usually require audited financial statements, but their form and content is left to management's preference.

Arbitrage Strictly speaking, arbitrage is the simultaneous buying and selling of the same thing in different markets without risk, in order to make a profit from the difference in price quotations between the markets. Recent practice has included "risk arbitrage," where the buying and selling are not simultaneous and there is some risk that the price difference will turn unprofitable. (A recent example has been buying *shares* in the stock market, expecting a *take-over* offer at a higher price.) When an *underwritten public offering* is expected for a company that already has shares in the *trading market*, the arbitrageurs will sometimes sell the shares short, that is, place sell orders for shares they do not yet own. This drives the market price down. As the *effective date* approaches, the lower market price causes the *underwriters* to negotiate for a reduced *offering price*. The arbitrageurs then buy shares in the *underwriting* to cover their short sales. Where there is no existing market, these short sales may occur in a *when-as-and-if-issued market*. In a *direct public offering*, the offering price will have been set before any public filing or announcement. As a result, the effect of selling pressure in the trading market would be to cause a postponement of the offering. The company can also remove the incentive for arbitrage by setting a maximum on the number of shares anyone may purchase in the offering.

Asked price Shares traded in the *over-the-counter market* will have prices quoted by their *market makers*, either on *NASDAQ* or in the *Pink Sheets*. The quotations are for the *bid price* (what the market maker will pay to buy at least 100 shares), or the asked price (what it will take to sell shares). For *listed shares*, bid and asked quotations are channeled through a *specialist*, a *dealer* who does business at a post on the *stock exchange* trading floor.

Auditors A firm of certified public accountants, independent of the company, that reviews the company's financial statements for the purpose of issuing an opinion on their fairness. Most *public offerings* of *securities* require audited financials.

Backdooring In some *underwritten initial public offerings*, speculators will commit to buy *shares* at the *offering price*, then immediately sell the same shares back through another *broker*. If it is a *hot new issue*, the price will have jumped up in the *aftermarket*, so the speculator makes a fast profit as a *flipper* of the shares. If the market reception has been cool, the speculator's shares will likely be sold "through the back door" to the *underwriting syndicate*, which has committed to buy shares for *stabilization* of the aftermarket price.

Bad boys Past offenders under *securities fraud* laws. When the *SEC* has authorized exemptions from full *registration statements*, such as *Regulation A* and *SCOR*, it prevents their use by a corporation affiliated with persons who have, within the previous five years, been convicted of *securities* fraud or who are subject to any enforcement order by a securities regulator. Filings under the securities laws require disclosure of bad boy affiliations.

Bedbug letter A major part of any *public offering* of *securities* is compliance with federal and state securities laws. Usually, this requires filing a *registration statement* with the *SEC* and receiving a letter of comment (*deficiency letter*). When the regulatory reviewers consider the company or its registration statement to have problems that can not be fixed by recommended changes, they suggest that the registration statement be withdrawn. This bad news is called a bedbug letter.

Best efforts underwriting When a *securities firm* agrees to use its "best efforts" to sell *shares* as an agent for the company. It is not technically an *underwriting* since that term means buying all the shares offered and reselling them to investors (see *firm commitment underwriting*). As a practical matter, most *underwritten initial public offerings* have become like best efforts. They are called *all-or-none offerings*, since the *underwriter* is not legally bound to buy the shares until it has collected *indications of interest* for the entire offering (as well as an additional margin of shares to cover sales to investors who *renege* after they receive their *confirmation*). Most best efforts agency agreements will have a minimum as well as a maximum number of shares that must be sold within the offering period. If the minimum is not met, the offering is cancelled and all money collected from investors is returned.

Beta A measure of a company's share price volatility—how wide the ups and downs of its trading price will be compared to the market generally. *Stock market* averages, like the Standard & Poor's 500, will be assigned the number 1.00 to reflect how much it would move on news about earnings, dividends, new products, etc. *Shares* of a very stable, mature company might move even less on that news, having a beta of, for instance, 0.74. On the other hand, an *emerging growth company*, especially in a competitive new technology or market, could have a beta of 2.00 or more.

Bid price The price at which the bidder will buy a specified number of *shares* (see *asked price*).

Big Six The largest international independent public accounting and consulting firms. Recent consolidations have reduced the "Big Eight" to these six: Arthur Andersen, Coopers & Lybrand, Deloitte & Touche, Ernst & Young, KMPG Peat Marwick, and Price Waterhouse.

Blind Pool Also known as "blank check" *public offerings*. These offerings are made without any specific business described for use of the offering *proceeds*.

Blue sky laws Nearly every state has its own securities regulators with whom a filing must be made for any *public offering* of *securities* to its residents. The governing laws were enacted to stop offerings that had no more substance behind them than "the blue sky." There are great differences among the states in their blue sky requirements—

both in the standards they impose and the detail work necessary to *qualify* an offering. Many are so-called *merit states*, where the regulatory staff actually judges the quality of the company and the terms of its share offering. The standard for most merit states is that the proposed investment be *fair, just and equitable* to the local citizens. Only limited coordination exists among the states (through *NASAA*) and the *SEC*, so that companies will have to consider blue sky costs and delays when designing their marketing program. The SEC has allowed offerings up to $1 million to occur without registration; several states now permit them to have simplified blue sky qualification under the *SCOR* or *ULOR* program.

Board of directors The governing body of a corporation which sets policy and appoints major officers. *Directors* are elected by the *shareowners*.

Bonds Debt *securities* generally for borrowings due to be repaid several years after they are issued. Bonds are legal instruments to evidence borrowed money. They are generally marketable *securities* and many are listed on *stock exchanges*. Corporate bonds are often subject to an *indenture*. There is no standardization among bonds; investors need to study the bond terms, as well as the credit and prospects of the corporate issuer. Bonds of large corporations are usually rated by Moody's or Standard & Poor's.

Book value The amount of a corporation's *shareowners' equity*. Also called *net worth*. Literally, the company's value according to its own accounting records. In many businesses, accounting methods and fluctuations in market value make the book value of academic interest only.

Bought deal When an *investment banker* or other intermediary has arranged for the purchase of an issue of *securities*, before offering to buy them from the issuer. This has become a frequent way for large corporations to sell securities, particularly debt. They can use a *shelf offering*, so that the issue is legally ready for immediate *public offering* and then wait to be approached with a bought deal.

Bracket underwriters *Securities firms* with the ability to be *managing underwriters* are arranged by tacit understanding into brackets. This explains the pyramid of alphabetical listings in the *tombstone ad* announcing a *public offering*. The rankings are based upon the number and stature of their corporate clients, their ability to originate new financial products, their coverage of *institutional investor* customers, and the number of their *registered representatives*. From four to seven firms at any one time seem to be at the top—the "bulge" or "special" bracket. Next is the "major" bracket, composed of most other large Wall Street firms. There was, at a point, a large "submajor" bracket of medium-sized Wall Street brokerages dealing primarily with individuals; these are now gone. A "mezzanine" bracket remains, consisting of Wall Street speciality houses and a few active underwriters in other cities. In the bottom bracket are the "regionals," that is, firms with offices only in one section of the country (with a small presence in New York).

Breaking the syndicate During a period after the *effective date*, *underwriters* can conduct *stabilization* activities. These usually involve placing buy orders at the *offering price* and accepting any offers to sell back *shares* purchased in the *underwriting*. The *agreement among underwriters* provides the authority for these transactions and spreads their cost among *underwriting syndicate* members. That authority terminates 30 days after the effective date unless the *managing underwriter* decides to shorten or extend it, usually by breaking the syndicate before the 30 days is over and letting the shares seek their market price in the *aftermarket*.

Broker Defined in the securities laws as a person in the business of buying and selling *securities* for the accounts of others. In everyday usuage, "broker" or "stockbroker" refers to an individual who talks with investors about their investments and causes their buy or sell orders to be executed. This may be a *registered representative* of a *securities firm*, an independent *broker-dealer*, or a *financial planner*.

Broker-assisted *Direct public offerings* can be successful without using any commissioned sales people. However, the size of the offering, its timing, or other factors may suggest using licensed *brokers* to sell part of the offering. They can be allocated a portion of the *shares* to sell on a *best efforts* basis to their own customers or by *cold calling* to *prospects* they generate. Or, the company can deliver the names and telephone numbers of people who have requested a *prospectus* to selected brokers and pay a negotiated commission rate for their *conversion* into sales.

Broker-dealer Individuals who have passed an examination and have met other standards can be licensed as a broker-dealer principal. This gives them and their corporate employer the right to engage in the business of buying and selling *securities*, both for the accounts of others (a *broker*) and for their own account (a *dealer*).

Brokerage firm The business organization which operates under a *broker-dealer* license, more often and accurately called a *securities firm*. Before the 1960s they were nearly all partnerships. Now they operate primarily as corporations, either publicly owned or as the subsidiary of a large insurance company or conglomerate.

Caller ID service Using a telephone company central office switch and an inexpensive computer system, a customer's file can be automatically displayed on a monitor as the customer is calling in (or as an outbound call is being placed). Where available, this service can improve *conversions*, particularly from inbound *telemarketing*. The monitor can display the caller's name, address, dates of the *response* and *fulfillment*, caller's priority for the marketing program, and all *demographic* information accumulated.

Capital Also known as capitalization. The amount of long-term money available to the company. The total of *shareowner* investment, earnings retained in the business, and borrowings which will not come due for more than a year. By the mechanics of double entry bookkeeping, capital is equal to assets minus short-term debt (due within a year).

Equity capital or *equity* is that part of the company's capital that comes from shareowner investment and retained earnings. It is more often called *net worth* or *shareowner's equity*.

Capital formation The process of adding to a company's *capital*. It usually refers to issuing equity or debt *securities*.

Certain transactions When money or property has passed between the company and one of its *insiders*, it may require explanation in the *prospectus*. The name, certain transactions, comes from the instructions accompanying the *SEC* forms for registering a *public offering*. For example, when an entrepreneur hopes to take a company public, it is wise to avoid any of the situations that would need description in the certain transactions section. They may make it difficult to *qualify* the offering under the *blue sky laws* of a *merit state*. Descriptions of certain transactions tend to be lengthy and complicated, causing *prospects* to reject the offering based on their "smell test."

Cheap shares When *insiders* have invested in the company within three years before the *public offering*, the amount they paid will be compared with the *offering price* to the public. A big difference raises the *cheap shares* issue, which must be dealt with satisfactorily for the public offering to be cleared through *SEC* and state *blue sky laws*. A *NASAA* Statement of Policy defines "cheap stock" (*shares*) and provides for their escrow as a condition to *qualify* the public offering in some states. While in escrow the shares can not be traded. Release from escrow is typically conditioned upon meeting a three-year earnings test (see *Promotional shares*).

Closing In an *underwriting*, the company delivers *share* certificates and the *underwriters* pay for the shares they have sold, less their commissions and expenses. The *closing* date is generally a week after the *effective date* of the underwriting. In a *direct public offering* there will be a date when the offering closes and no more orders are accepted. An allocation is then made when more shares have been ordered than were offered, and certificates are mailed to the new *shareowners*.

Cold calling When a *broker* or agent makes telephone solicitations to strangers, usually from a list of *prospects*. Securities laws require a *prospectus* to be delivered before *shares* can be sold so cold calling can only be for gathering *indications of interest* in the shares.

Cold comfort Sometimes called "negative comfort." A representation made by someone independent of the company, to the effect that although they have not checked everything, what they did check revealed nothing wrong. The company's *auditors* are required to give the *underwriters* a "cold comfort letter" just before the *underwriting agreement* is signed. It lists several pages of "special procedures" the auditors have performed. The letter explains that this was not an audit and finally, gives the cold comfort that "nothing came to our attention that caused us to believe that" there are any misleading errors or omissions in the material reviewed. Getting this letter is part of the underwriters' *due diligence* defense against claims by investors who lose money on their investment.

Common shares Also known as common stock. These are the basic units of ownership in a corporation. Their voting rights elect the *board of directors*, which sets policy and hires and fires management. When a corporation is sold or liquidated, whatever is left, after paying off creditors and any senior securities, belongs to the owners of common shares. Some corporations have more than one class of common shares, usually as a way to keep voting control in the founders' family.

Confirmation Shares are sold in an *underwriting* when *brokers* telephone their customers and *prospects*. Since this takes place a week or so before the *effective date*, there is no final *prospectus* available. Securities laws require delivery of a prospectus before a "sale." That means when an investor agrees to buy, it is called an *indication of interest* or "circling a number of shares." Then, on the effective date the prospectus is mailed to the investor along with a confirmation showing the company's name, number of *shares*, and amount due in payment. The investor either pays on the *settlement date* or *reneges* on the sale.

Control person Securities laws place potential liability for investor losses onto persons who "control" the company. They include executive officers, *directors*, and the owners of more than five percent of the company's *shares*. Control persons are *insiders* subject to special rules about trading in the company's shares and passing on information about the company that would be important to a decision about buying or selling its shares.

Conversion A *direct public offering* follows the steps of *direct marketing*: (1) the *proposition* (offer to provide a *prospectus*), (2) the *prospects' response* in requesting the prospectus, (3) *fulfillment* through delivery of the prospectus, and then (4) *conversion* of the prospects into *share-owners*.

Corporate cleanup When a company is owned by an entrepreneur, it may be used to minimize taxes. Its structure may reflect negotiations with *angel investors* or *venture capitalists*. There can be a certain casualness about corporate proceedings. When presented to the public and the securities regulators, the business should be simple, tidy, and as independent as practicable. This transformation is called corporate cleanup and calls for some balance among the securities lawyer, marketing advisor, and management.

Corporate governance Corporations are much like the British form of government with each *share* similar to one registered voter. Shares elect *directors*. The *board of directors* makes policy, appoints officers, and monitors their performance. The rights and responsibilities of *share-owners*, directors, and officers are determined by laws of the state from which the corporation has its charter.

CUSIP number All certificates for *publicly traded shares* require an identification known as a CUSIP number. They are issued by the New York office of Standard & Poor's Corporation, (212) 208-8331.

Customer information file or CIF Nearly every business maintains some sort of information about its customers. With such computer peripherals as bar code scanning, information can be gathered about buying patterns. Through access to data banks (available from *list brokers*, credit card companies, credit bureaus, and government registrations), a *CIF* can provide extensive statistics and *demographics* about customers. Because of their preexisting relationship, customers are usually *prospects* for a company's *shares* in a *direct public offering*.

Database enhancement Adding externally compiled information to the company's *customer information file*. There are suppliers who compile and sell statistics and *demographics* on nearly every adult American. Their data can be added for each name in the customer information file.

Database management Information management is a major part of any *direct public offering*. Information must be gathered, checked, and communicated in order for people to make an investment decision. In addition, information about the people to whom the shares will be offered must also be acquired and used. Database management includes names, addresses, telephone numbers, and other useful facts about selected individuals and markets. Some of this data may be purchased, some developed from responses to advertising, and some built from the company's own records as well as the knowledge of its employees and advisors. Database management handles the arranging of that data into categories reflecting the probabilities of investment in certain amounts. It enables the sorting and displaying of data in the most useful form for selecting *media*, preparing messages, doing *telemarketing*, and tracking results.

Dealer Securities laws define a dealer as one who buys and sells *securities* for the dealer's own account. This contrasts with a *broker* who buys and sells as the agent for others. In the 1930s, Congress had almost decreed that each *securities firm* could be either a broker or a dealer, but not both. The reason was to separate giving advice to customers from also being an investor. Instead, the standard license in the business is a "registered broker-dealer." *Underwriters* are dealers, since they technically buy the *shares* from the company and resell them to investors.

Deficiency letter Often called a "letter of comment." When a *registration statement* has been filed with the *SEC* or a state securities administrator, it will generate a list of comments from the staff assigned to its review. There are usually separate ones for the text and the financial statements. The process generally involves comparing the filing with the most recent ones the agency has cleared for similar businesses. Since the law does not call upon the SEC to pass upon the adequacy of a registration statement, the comments are only "suggestions." Failure to make changes or otherwise explain each matter may mean that the registration statement never becomes effective and the offering is cancelled. Sometimes the staff will send a *bedbug letter*, telling the company that its registration statement is considered so deficient that it cannot be fixed with an amendment.

Delaying amendment When a *registration statement* is on file with the *SEC*, it would automatically reach an *effective date* and be usable to sell securities. To prevent this, securities lawyers routinely include a *delaying amendment* in the filing. They then request *acceleration* of the effective date to a selected time.

Demographics The use of population statistics to classify *prospects* by particular characteristics. *Customer information files* often have little information beyond name, address, and telephone number. When lists are purchased, they are often subscribers to particular magazines, purchasers from designated catalogs, or contributors to selected fundraisers. At its most basic level, demographics is the selection of *target markets* by the ZIP code of their residence, which is some indication of household wealth. Much more demographic information can be added to these files and lists through *database enhancement*. Census data now encourages "geodemographics," the correlation of location with the propensity to invest. So much information is available from credit bureaus and customer information files, that the science has moved on to "psychographics," where a mix of data bits will suggest spending patterns and other characteristics useful in planning and executing a marketing program.

Dilution Whenever new shares are issued, there is some financial effect upon the company's existing *shareowners*. This is usually measured by the increase or decrease in the amount of *shareowners' equity*, or *book value* per *share*. A decrease in book value per share occurs when the proceeds from each new share sold are less than the company's *shareowners' equity*, which is then divided by the number of shares existing before the sale. (For instance, proceeds from a sale of new shares at $8.00 each would mean *dilution* for the owners of 10,000 existing shares of a company with a shareowners' equity of $100,000). When the proceeds of new shares exceed the book value of existing shares, the offering is considered "antidilutive." Dilution may also refer to the expected earnings or cash flow to come from the use of money received in the offering of new shares. If those earnings are not at least equal to current earnings per share before the sale, then there is dilution of earnings to the existing shareowners.

Direct mail One of the *media* used in *direct marketing*. A marketing *proposition* is sent by mail to a list of *prospects* who may communicate their *response* by mail, telephone, facsimile, or other media.

Direct marketing Some of its practitioners prefer "direct response marketing," and all of them abhor the label *direct mail* or worse, "junk mail." The concept is the same as *disintermediation* in the financial services industry— eliminating the businesses in the middle, dealing directly with the customer. In the language of direct marketing, the process for a *direct public offering* involves:

> The *proposition*: "We'll give you a *prospectus*."
> The *response*: "OK, I'd like to see it."
> The *fulfillment*: "Here is the prospectus."
> The *conversion*: "This is my order for *shares*."

Direct marketing has developed several generations beyond the first solicitations by mail to everyone in selected neighborhoods. Now it incorporates *demographics, database management, list brokers, fulfillment* houses, and *telemarketing* specialists. *Media* used still includes direct mail, but the proposition may also come through radio or television with responses communicated to an 800 *telemarketing* system. Fulfillment may be effected with a videotape or floppy disk containing the prospectus and *selling materials.* The conversion could be handled by facsimile transmission of an order form, with telephone or computer transfer of funds.

Direct public offering or *DPO.* Shares are sold by the company to investors through *direct marketing.* This contrasts with an *underwritten public offering* sold by *registered representatives* who work for *securities firms* in an *underwriting syndicate.*

Directed sales In an *underwritten public offering,* a *money manager* for *institutional investors* will often ask the *managing underwriter* to take an order for *shares* and give credit for the sale to a particular *securities firm.* The designated firm will then be paid the 60 percent *selling concession* portion of the *underwriting spread.* This is a way for money managers to pay *securities firms* for research or other services provided "free" under so-called *soft dollar deals.*

Directors Representatives elected by the *shareowners* to the *board of directors* who set policy and appoint executives.

Disintermediation When money is transferred directly between the user and the provider without passing through a *financial intermediary.* An example has been the commercial paper market, where large corporations lend and borrow among themselves, rather than through bank deposits and bank loans. A *direct public offering* is a form of disintermediation because there is no underwriter.

Disk Marketing Delivering the *direct marketing fulfillment* on a floppy disk for computer access by the *prospect*. Providing the *prospectus* and *selling materials* on a disk allows the prospects to use their own programs to compare, project, and analyze the information.

Dividends Payments of amounts per *share* by a corporation to its *shareowners*. Dividends represent a proportion of the corporation's earnings (except for liquidating dividends and other unusual cases). They are usually paid in cash, but may be newly issued additional shares. Sometimes, the shares of a subsidiary or other corporate assets are distributed to shareowners as a dividend.

Dog and pony show The *road show* arranged by *underwriters* for *money managers* who are *prospects* for an *underwritten public offering*.

Due diligence Securities laws allow disappointed investors to recover their losses in court from persons related to the company or involved in a *public offering* of its *shares*. One of the ways to avoid that liability is known as the due diligence defense. It requires that the defendant make a reasonable investigation into the truth and completeness of the *registration statement*.

EDGAR The *SEC*'s Electronic Data Gathering, Analysis and Retrieval system for companies to file documents by computer media. This is part of the very slow progress into the electronic age. When the pilot project becomes fully operational, investors will be able to retrieve data in real time for use in their own analysis.

Effective date This is the precise moment when the *registration statement* "becomes effective" with the *SEC* and state agencies. Only then can the *prospectus* be used in offering *shares* to the public. In an *underwriting*, timing of the effective date will have been requested by the lawyers to come at the point when the sales efforts are concluded by the *underwriters' brokers*. If those efforts have been successful and the company agrees to the underwriters' final price, the *underwriting agreement* will be signed a few hours before the effective date. Then, confirmations of the sale are sent to investors with a copy of the prospectus. In a *direct public offering*, the sales program really begins on the effective date. The final prospectus is sent to those who have requested it by responding to ads or public relations efforts. An order form accompanies the prospectus, often as a detachable page.

Emerging growth company The definition of *growth company* is a business beyond the start-up phase but not yet mature. The term *emerging growth company*, is used to describe a business that is just coming out of start-up and entering the growth company category. Most candidates for an *initial public offering* are emerging growth companies.

Emerging growth stock A popular term to describe shares of companies large enough to have a *trading market*, but still in the early stages of an expected period of growth. They usually have *price/earnings ratios* higher than market averages because investors are paying for the discounted present value of expected future earnings and cash flow. These expectations often change as events unfold, causing the stock price to fluctuate more than market averages (see *Beta*).

ERISA The Employee Retirement Income Security Act of 1974. It cast into stone the "herd instinct" of *money managers* who invest for pension funds by redefining the common-law "prudent investor" rule. Congress changed the fiduciary duty from investing other people's money as the manager would invest its own, to investing the same way as other *institutional investors*. This standard gets tested every quarter when money managers file public reports. One effect has been to turn the *stock market* and *securities firms* into a short-term performance race. This has largely discouraged *individual investors* from buying or holding *shares*. *Direct public offerings* can operate outside the securities markets dominated by ERISA investors.

ESOPs Employee Stock Ownership Plans are trusts set up to own a company's *shares* for the benefit of its employees. The legal structure was a creation of the Internal Revenue Code sixty years ago and Congress has recently added several tax incentives for companies to form ESOPs. They have also been used to put large blocks of *publicly traded shares* into the hands of a trustee who will protect management from a *takeover*. In most cases employees cannot vote, sell, or receive *dividends* on the shares. Their interest in the trust is cashed out when they leave the company. Most ESOPs have been created with bank borrowings which must be repaid out of the company's cash flow.

Endorsement A marketing message that uses someone outside the company to express approval of the product or service being sold. A "testimonial" is usually a favorable quotation from an individual who is either famous or someone with whom the *prospects* are expected to identify. Other endorsements are more subtle. Advertising in a particular *media* may connote its endorsement, especially if other advertisers are well known. A powerful endorsement for a *direct public offering* can come from a *sponsor*, especially one making a *standby commitment*—a promise to buy any *shares* not purchased by prospects.

Equity In finance and accounting this term means the owner's investment in the business. It is used interchangeably with *shareowners' equity* or *net worth*. It includes amounts the owners have invested, plus or minus the earnings or losses that have been accumulated from operating the business.

Exempt securities Federal and state securities laws read as if they applied to all *securities*. They then define certain kinds as being exempt securities, to which the registration, disclosure, and some antifraud provisions of the laws do not apply. These include securities of certain types of organizations like banks and government agencies.

Exempt transactions Securities laws apply to every purchase and sale of *securities*, unless a specific exemption applies. Most *stock market* transactions are exempt, as are *private placements*. The *SEC* and the courts keep the interpretation of exempt transactions rather narrow. It can be dangerous to sell *shares* without a *no-action letter* or an opinion of counsel that the proposed transaction is within *SEC safe harbor* rules or other defined limits.

Fair, just and equitable State *blue sky laws* often require their enforcement agency to pass upon the quality of the proposed offering of *shares* to residents. These are the *merit states* and a frequent standard is that the terms of the proposed offering, the investment itself, and the method of sale are all fair, just and equitable to the local residents. Where the offering is limited to *prospects* meeting certain standards (usually wealth and income), the agency may also pass upon the *suitability* of the investment for that class of investors.

Fair price provision Language in the corporation's charter requiring that all *shareowners* receive the same price in any *takeover* of a controlling interest in the *shares*. This prevents the "two-tier" offer, where the first group of shares tendered in acceptance of the offer receives one price, while the remaining shares get a lower price in a later offer. The *fair price provision* may not be a particularly effective *shark repellant*, but it does protect shareowners who hold their shares in *street name* or are otherwise slow in responding to a takeover offer.

FASB (pronounced "fazby") The Financial Accounting Standards Board—an attempt to bring uniformity and understanding to generally accepted accounting principles (*GAAP*).

Filing date The day on which a *registration statement* for a *public offering* is filed with the *SEC* (or a filing is made to *qualify* under state *blue sky laws*). It marks the end of the *prefiling period* and the beginning of the *waiting period*.

Financial intermediary Someone in between the company which wants money to use and the source of that money. Banks get money from depositors and lend it to businesses.

Securities firms channel money from investors to corporations by selling *securities. Disintermediation* occurs when the money flows directly from the source to the company, as in a *direct public offering.*

Financial planner An advisor to individuals in their financial affairs. Financial planners will review their clients' income, expenses, assets, debts, tax status, and future needs. Then they may recommend a budget and the purchase of financial products, like insurance or investments. There is little special government licensing or regulation of financial planners. Most of them are licensed to sell insurance or *securities* and earn their living from commissions on sales. Some are "fee-only" financial planners who accept no commissions and are compensated solely by an agreed fee or percentage of their client's assets or investment income. Sometimes this includes incentive arrangements for investment results above performance standards. Fee-only financial planners who have a large practice become subject to the federal Investment Advisers Act of 1940 and similar state laws. They are then usually called *investment advisors* or *money managers.*

Financial printers Printing businesses that specialize in printing documents used in corporate or government finance, such as *prospectuses, annual reports,* and *takeover* offers. What distinguishes them from commercial printers is the intensive level of service—speed, accuracy, and responsiveness to nearly every whim of the company's securities lawyers. There is, of course, an extra price for this service. Word processing, especially computer telecommunications and desktop publishing, make it possible for cooperative lawyers, *auditors,* and other advisors to perform everything but large-scale print runs, eliminating the need for a financial printer. As a consequence of these changes and the general slowdown in corporate finance transactions, there are only three national survivors: Bowne, Donnelley and Merrill.

Finder A person who introduces a company to a source of financing—an investor or another *financial intermediary,* like a bank or *securities firm*. Finders typically get paid a fee upon *closing* of the financing.

Firm commitment underwriting A *public offering* of *securities* by an *underwriting syndicate*, where the *underwriting agreement* contains a firm commitment by the *underwriters* to buy all of the shares. In practice, the underwriting agreement is not signed until *indications of interest* have been gathered by *brokers* for sales of more than all the *shares*. Large, older *securities firms* will usually participate only in firm commitment underwritings and not in *best efforts underwritings*.

First refusal rights Some *IPO underwriters* will require that they be given the right to be the company's *investment banker* and receive a fee on future corporate finance transactions. They will have no obligation, but will have the first refusal rights to any proposed arrangement with a *securities firm*.

Flipper There is potential for a "heads-I-win, tails-you-lose" game in *underwritten initial public offerings*. Members of the *underwriting syndicate* will have signed an *agreement among underwriters*, which binds them to buy back shares at the *offering price* for *stabilization* of the *aftermarket*, for a period as long as 60 days after the *effective date* of the *underwriting*. A flipper will buy the shares in the offering, then sell them back within the next few hours or days. On a *hot new issue*, the flipper realizes a quick profit by selling to someone who did not get shares in the underwriting and is willing to pay more for them in the aftermarket. If the price does not go up, the flipper can resell shares back to the underwriting syndicate (often by *backdooring* through another *broker*). The only cost to the flipper is the brokerage fee on the resale, since the *underwriters* have fixed a floor price. Even that can be profitable for the flipper because of a *soft dollar deal*, where part of the *underwriting spread* is credited to the flipper.

Float This has two very different meanings. As a noun, the float is the number of a company's *shares* that are owned by the public, rather than owned by the company's officers, directors, and other *insiders*. A minimum float is required by a *stock exchange* for *listed shares* and by *NASDAQ* for its price quotation system. As a verb, to float shares means to sell a *new issue* through an *underwriting*. The British refer to an *underwritten public offering* as a "flotation."

Focus group A *market research* tool. A dozen or so individuals, who are thought to be representative of the *target markets* for a *direct public offering*, are invited to meet as a group for two or three hours. Payment is made to them or a designated charity. Trained facilitators ask questions and monitor a discussion of the investment *proposition* and marketing methods. Company officers and advisors watch through a one-way mirror, and the session is usually recorded by audio or videotape.

Founders' shares Before businesses go public, their *shares* are often owned by the entreprenuer and other *private placement* investors. The question will be raised of *dilution* and *promotional shares*. Depending upon the difference between the price paid for founders' shares and the *offering price* to the public, special disclosure in the *prospectus* may be required under *SEC* rules. If the private placement was made within three years before the proposed *public offering*, the *blue sky laws* in *merit states* may require an escrow of the *cheap shares*, or even prohibit the sale to their residents as unfair.

Free-riding When shares of a *hot new issue* are purchased by *securities firms* for their own account (or for their employees and their immediate families), rather than for distribution to the public. *NASD* rules prohibit free-riding, but they do not prevent favored customers from getting all the shares available in the *underwriting* or upon exercise of the *Green shoe* option.

Free writing period From the *effective date* to the conclusion of the *public offering*. *Shares* may be offered only by a final *prospectus*, which is available only after the *effective date* of the *SEC* registration. Any other communication, in writing or on radio or video, may be considered a prospectus in violation of the securities laws. But, during the *free writing period*, other *selling materials* may be used if accompanied or preceded by the final prospectus. When preparing a *time and responsibility schedule*, the *fulfillment* (delivery of the prospectus to *prospects*) should come immediately after the *effective date*. It can then be accompanied with other *selling materials* and followed with additional marketing tools.

Fulfillment In *direct marketing* terms this occurs when a *prospectus* is sent in *fulfillment* of a *prospect's response* to the company's *proposition*—that it would furnish a free prospectus.

Fully diluted Per share earnings or other amounts in a company's financial statements after giving effect to the potential issuance of additional *shares*. This occurs when a company has issued *warrants* or *options* to purchase shares in the future, often as incentives to employees or investors, or as compensation to an *investment banker* or other *financial intermediary*.

GAAP (pronounced "gap") An acronym for generally accepted accounting principles, which must be observed in financial statements in order to get a clean opinion from the company's *auditors*—a necessity in virtually every *public offering*. Conforming to GAAP may be painful for an entrepreneur if the company's bookkeeping has principally served to save on taxes.

Glass-Steagall The Banking Act of 1933, which separated commercial banks from *investment bankers* and prohibited commercial banks or their affiliates from *underwriting securities*. Because an underwriting is technically an investment in securities and a resale, the *underwriter* must have *capital* to cover a prescribed ratio to the amount of the underwriting. Taking banks out of the business severely limited the number of investment bankers which had sufficient capital to do underwritings. The Federal Reserve Board of Governors has been gradually relaxing the Glass-

Steagall restrictions, most recently permitting certain banks to form holding company affiliates to act as underwriters of corporate debt and equity securities. In a *direct public offering*, because there is no underwriting, commercial banks are free to act as advisor. Their *broker-dealer* affiliates can also be agents in the *conversion* of *prospects* into *shareowners*.

Go public When a company owned by no more than a few *shareowners* comes to have *publicly traded shares*. The usual method is through an *initial public offering*.

Go public by the back door When a business comes to have *publicly traded shares* without an *initial public offering*. This can happen through a series of acquisitions of businesses, paying the former owners in new shares of the acquiring corporation. It may result from a string of *private placements* with a gradual widening of shareownership until a *trading market* develops. A third way for a business to go public by the back door is for *promoters* to organize or acquire a *shell corporation* which already has publicly traded shares, or does a blind pool offering. Then the shell acquires the operating business.

Golden parachute An employment contract, requiring a significant amount of severance pay for an officer or director in the event of a hostile *takeover* of the company. Golden parachutes are often justified as assuring the *shareowners* that officers and directors will not block an otherwise favorable acquisition in order to save their jobs.

Green Shoe In a *firm commitment underwriting*, the *underwriting syndicate* agrees to buy a fixed number of *shares* from the company. The selling efforts will have been concluded before the *underwriting agreement* is signed by *registered representatives* gathering telephone *indications of interest* from their customers and *prospects*. Some of these buyers will *renege* by refusing to accept and pay for the *shares*. Other buyers will be *flippers* who force the underwriting syndicate to buy back shares as part of their aftermarket price *stabilization*. To protect against this, underwriting syndicates takes orders for considerably more *shares* than are included in the *underwriting* (similar to the overbooking of airline reservations in anticipation of cancellations and "no-shows"). But if more shares have to be delivered to buyers than are included in the underwriting agreement, the *underwriters* could be required to cover the shortage through buying shares in the *aftermarket*. This would likely drive the trading price up, causing losses to the underwriting syndicate. In an underwriting for the Green Shoe Manufacturing Company, underwriters first negotiated an option to cover these *overallotments* by buying more shares from the company (or its major *shareowners*) within 30 days after the *effective date*. The first Green Shoe options were for up to ten percent of the shares underwritten. The maximum is now commonly fifteen percent and the most frequent use of the Green Shoe is to reward the underwriters' favored clients by getting them *hot new issues* at the original *offering price*. (*NASD* rules against *free-riding* prevent underwriters from themselves investing in hot new issues.)

Growth company This term is an attempt to classify businesses that are not yet "mature," but are beyond the "start-up" phase. Mature companies are in markets that are not expected to get much larger (like some public utilities), or have products that nearly everyone owns and will only replace when worn out (for example, refrigerators). They usually have a low risk of failure and a low potential for major growth. Start-ups are very high risk, and if they succeed, can produce rapid growth in size and share value.

Gun-jumping Rules of the *SEC* and state *blue sky laws* limit the advertising and publicity that can appear before the *effective date* and the delivery of a *prospectus* to each of the offering's *prospects*. If these rules are violated through gun-jumping, the offering may have to be postponed for a "cooling-off period," or even cancelled. In the words of the SEC, gun-jumping is publicity or other communications that "may in fact contribute to conditioning the public mind or arousing public interest in the issuer or in the securities of an issuer in a manner which raises a serious question whether the publicity is not in fact part of the selling effort." SEC Rule 135 permits a very limited prefiling public announcement of a proposed offering.

Hot new issue An *underwritten initial public offering* that trades in the immediate *aftermarket* at a price higher than the *offering price*. According to rules of the *NASD*, member firms and their employees may not trade in hot new issues.

Incubators Start-up businesses are typically financed on a shoestring. They need cheap quarters and they need lots of experienced advice for "free." Incubators are usually sponsored by universities or community development organizations. They provide space for several beginning businesses, pool support services, and provide consultation all at a cost that is usually below market value. Several incubators are also tied in with groups of *informal investors*, from whom tenants may be able to raise capital.

Indenture The contract among a company, investors, and a trustee, governing the issuance of corporate *bonds*. These are generally very long and must be filed with the *SEC* under the Trust Indenture Act of 1939.

Indications of interest When *brokers* write orders for *shares* in an *initial public offering*. No sale of shares can occur until the *effective date* and delivery of a final *prospectus* to the customer. In practice, the prospectus in an *underwritten IPO* is first sent to the customer when it accompanies the confirmation of sale. The customer then has five days to pay for the shares at the *offering price*, or to *renege* and cancel the order.

Individual investors People who are investing their own money directly. Included are IRAs and trusts for family members. Not included are people who channel their money through mutual funds, pension plans, or other *institutional investors*.

Influentials People who influence the decisions of others. Members of the community to whom acquaintances turn for advice or a role model because of their position, reputation, or personality. A *direct public offering* program will try to reach these people first.

Infomercial Also known as "infocommercial." A commercial message presented like a feature story. Most advertisements are short and in a rather standardized format, whether the *media* is print or electronic. An infomercial is longer and packaged to resemble news, editorial copy, or programming. There will be some distinguishable mark, like the word "advertisement" in print or a voice-over in television: "This special announcement is brought to you by . . . "

Informal investors Also known as *angel investors*. There is a period between the start-up of most businesses and their *initial public offering* when capital is needed to become established and profitable. These businesses will probably not be attractive to *venture capital firms*, most of which have become institutionalized and unwilling to take risks on little companies. As a result, various networks of informal investors have developed all over the country. They are often coordinated by *incubators*, accounting firms, or management consultants.

Initial public offering (IPO) For a corporation, the *initial public offering* is like a coming-of-age rite. It signals that a company has joined the ranks of successful businesses. As a matter of practical finance, the first-time sale of *shares* to the public opens the door to large amounts of *capital* with no interest expense, no repayment, and no restrictive covenants on management. For the founders and early investors it places a market value on their investment and provides the *liquidity* for some cash return. In the past nearly every IPO was a *firm commitment underwriting* through an *underwriting syndicate*. Today the developments in *direct marketing* make possible the *direct public offering (DPO)*.

Internal memoranda A brief writing, video, or audio tape used to tell *registered representatives* about the offering and give them selling points for their *telemarketing*. It is unlawful to show internal memoranda to *prospects*.

Insider A person in a position to control the corporation or to have access to nonpublic information which, if publicly known, would likely affect the price of the *shares*. The legal definition varies with the particular legal duty involved. Insider trading is periodically the subject of prosecution and publicity.

Institutional investors Pools of capital under the control of *money managers*. The largest institutional investors are pension funds, insurance companies, mutual funds, and endowments for schools and religious bodies. Nearly half the *shares* of America's largest corporations are owned by institutional investors. Because they buy and sell investments much more frequently than individual *investors*, over 70 percent of the trading in corporate *shares* is done for institutional investors. After years of poor performance, money managers of many pension plans have been replaced by index managers who invest in the same shares and proportions as the Standard & Poor's 500 or other market indexes. In recent years, most *underwritten IPOs* have been sold to institutional investors and individual speculators.

Interactive marketing This occurs when the company and the *prospects* can communicate back and forth immediately, without the delay of going from a *proposition* in one *media* (newspaper or TV) to a *response* in another (telephone or mail) and on to a *fulfilment* and *conversion*. The oldest interactive marketing (as well as the most costly and time-consuming) is calling upon *prospects* in person or by telephone. Electronic means of interactive marketing include facsimile machines, computer modems, and *videotex*.

Intrastate exemption Registration of a *public offering* with the *SEC* is not required if the *shares* are offered and sold only to residents of the same state in which the company is incorporated, has its headquarters, and does nearly all of its business. Most securities lawyers are nervous about recommending use of this exemption since the SEC or the courts may challenge it. If only one offeree or investor is not a resident, or if a buyer resells to a nonresident within the next nine months, the exemption is lost.

Investment advisor Technically, a person or firm registered under the federal Investment Advisers Act of 1940 or similar state law. (The preferred modern spelling has become "advisor," rather than "adviser.") Under *ERISA*, investment advisors are really *money managers*, having been delegated the absolute decision-making authority to buy and sell investments, within some general guidelines. *Financial planners* may be registered investment advisors. Many are not because they operate on too small a scale to require registration.

Investment banker This is not a defined term under the securities laws, like *broker, dealer*, or *investment advisor*. It most often refers to the corporate finance department of a *securities firm* which handles *public offerings* and *private placements* of *securities*, as well as mergers, acquisitions, and other corporate finance transactions. Many securities firms call themselves investment bankers even when the only services they provide are as a broker for trading *securities* in the *secondary market*.

Investment company These are generally mutual funds regulated under the federal Investment Company Act of 1940. They are *institutional investors* run by *money managers*. Some of them have a specific investment objective that includes the purchase of *emerging growth shares*, often through an *initial public offering*.

Investment letter Legal documents used in a *private placement* of *securities* to avoid violating the laws requiring registration of a *public offering*. They state that the buyer is purchasing for investment purposes only and not with a view to the redistribution of the securities. The letter usually has the effect of a contract and may require that the securities be held for a particular period of time, that an opinion of counsel be obtained before any sale, or that the securities can only be transferred to a certain class of investors. *Shares* subject to an investment letter are known as *lettered stock*.

Issuer *Shares* come from a corporate issuer as fractional ownership interests. Corporations may also be the issuers of debt securities and *options* or *warrants*. For each share or other security, there is an issuer and an investor.

Issuer-directed shares In an *underwritten initial public offering*, every share must be sold through the *underwriters*. The entrepreneur and company management can request that shares be sold by the *underwriting syndicate* to persons who have some special relationship to the company, such as members of the board of directors. Some underwriters will not permit the practice and *NASD* rules allow only 10 percent of the shares to be issuer-directed. An *underwriting spread* must be paid on all *shares*, including any which are issuer-directed.

Junk bonds Long-term corporate debt *securities* are generally issued as *bonds*. Before the 1970s, nearly all bonds sold in *public offerings* were rated as to their investment quality by Moody's or Standard & Poor's. When the term junk bonds was coined, it referred to bonds of "fallen angels," corporations which had qualified for a rating when the bonds were issued, but had lost their rating when the business fell on hard times. The term carried over to the use of *new issues* of high-yield, unrated bonds for *growth companies* and acquisitions. One reason for the use of new junk bonds was the deduction from corporate income taxes allowed for interest payments on bonds, but not for dividends on *shares*. Another was the preference of *institutional investors* for *liquidity*. The *trading market* for shares of growth companies was often too thin to allow sales of large amounts without depressing the price. Junk bonds might be no more marketable, but they substituted an obligation to repay the investment in a few years and a high cash return until repayment. Since most institutional investors are tax-exempt, all of the interest received counted toward the return on investment. Junk bonds allowed *money* *managers* to show better short-term results than their peers, who invested in *stocks* or rated bonds. During the 1980s, junk bonds met the capital needs for *emerging growth companies* that have traditionally used *equity* to finance rapid growth.

Know-your-customer rule *Securities firms* and *brokers* are subject to certain standards of conduct under securities laws, *self-regulatory organization* rules, and court decisions. One such standard they should know about is their customers' financial condition and needs before recommending a transaction. The *broker* can then determine the *suitability* of the proposed transaction for the customer.

Lead underwriter When there are multiple *managing underwriters*, one of them takes the lead and "runs the books" for the *underwriting syndicate*. The *lead underwriter's* name will appear on the left side of the first line in the listing of underwriting syndicate members for the *tombstone ad.*

Legal opinion For an *initial public offering*, securites laws require an opinion of the company's lawyers for the benefit of investors in the *shares*. These are in standardized form and provide the lawyers' opinion that the shares have been legally issued.

Letter of intent When a corporation and a *managing underwriter* reach an understanding about doing an *initial public offering*, they sign a letter of intent. It describes the proposed *offering price*, number of *shares*, and *effective date*. An *underwriting spread* will be included, as well as an amount of *underwriters' warrants*. However, nothing in the letter of intent is legally binding, except a usual provision for the corporation to pay expenses if it calls off the deal.

Letter stock *Shares* acquired in a *private placement* where the investor has signed an *investment letter*. Because of the restrictions created on transfer of ownership, letter stock can be sold only to certain persons. As a result, the sales price will often be at a discount of 20 percent to 50 percent of a *trading market* price.

Leverage The ratio of borrowed money to *equity* capital in a business reflects its leverage. The concept is that a base of *equity* money can be enhanced in its power by debt *capital*. The amount of leverage considered prudent varies significantly by industry. Financial institutions, like banks, may be considered very sound if they have $12 of debt for every $1 of equity. Manufacturing businesses often have only $1 of debt for every $2 of equity. In 1983, equity was over 65 percent of the total capital of U.S. corporations. By 1989, the equity portion had dropped to about 52 percent. To get back to the historic average of 57.7 percent equity, American corporations would have to sell over $300 billion in *shares*. This process is referred to as "deleveraging."

List broker Lists of *prospects* are used for *direct mail* and *telemarketing*. They may come from magazine subscription or credit card records. Some are compiled from census data, others from credit reporting agencies or government registration files. A good list broker will help develop a profile of the company's prospects, then suggest lists that will *merge and purge* to most closely match that profile.

List maintenance Companies will develop their own lists of *prospects* for *direct public offerings* from *customer information files*, purchased lists, and other sources. Once these lists have been through a *merge and purge* program, they need to be kept current and secure through list maintenance procedures. Like *database enhancement*, list maintenance is part of a company's *database management*.

Listed shares *Shares* admitted for trading on a *stock exchange*. One *securities firm* will be appointed by the exchange to be the *specialist* in a company's shares and will process all *bid* and *asked* offers. (As the exchanges gradually automate, some orders will be matched electronically.)

Liquidity How quickly an asset can be converted into freely available cash. For a company, it is the proportion of its assets consisting of money in the bank, accounts receivable, salable inventory, and the like. For an investor, it means how long it would take to sell and collect cash without a resulting drop in market value.

Management's Discussion and Analysis (MD&A) In a *public offering* the securities laws generally require this section in the *prospectus. Annual reports* will also have an MD&A. It requires management to comment on changes in financial conditions and results for comparative recent periods, as well as such issues as *liquidity*, and the effect of laws for environmental protection.

Managing underwriter The *securities firm* that originates the proposed *public offering* and is responsible for both client relations and putting together the *underwriting syndicate.* As compensation, the managing underwriter receives 20 percent of the *underwriting spread*, as well as what it earns by participating in the *underwriting syndicate* and having its *brokers* sell *shares*. There are often multiple managing underwriters, in which case one will be the *lead manager* and "run the books" for the syndicate.

Market capitalization The number of *shares* a company has issued, multiplied by its market price per share.

Market maker A *securities firm* which quotes *bid* and *asked prices* for particular *shares* in the *over-the-counter market.* A market maker must generally be willing to buy at least 100 shares at its quoted bid and sell at least 100 shares at its quoted asked price.

Market out Also known as "catastrophe out." Conditions in an *underwriting agreement* giving the *underwriters* the right not to go through with an *underwritten public offering.* They are generally limited to such events as a suspension of the securities trading markets, a general banking moratorium, or a "material change in general economic, political, or financial conditions." As a practical matter, the underwriting agreement is not signed until hours before the *effective date* and orders for more than all the *shares* have been taken. As a result, the market out conditions only apply to events during the six days or so before the *closing*.

Market research This is the work done to determine whether a *direct public offering* is feasible, to select the best markets, and to suggest the most effective message and *media*. It is akin to "alpha testing" a new product before the *test marketing* or "beta testing" stage. Tools of market research include studying the case histories of other companies, *demographics*, interviews, questionnaires, and *focus groups*.

Market segmentation This is an effort to make marketing more cost-effective. In mass marketing, a message is delivered through a medium that includes far more people than those who are likely *prospects* for the product or service being offered. Most print and electronic *media* are priced on the basis of the number of people they reach without regard to their *demographic* or other characteristics. Screening for such factors as income level and age will often suggest media which are directed to the logical prospects.

Market timing *Shares* of each corporation have their individual price trends depending upon investors' estimates of the corporation's future profitability and growth. Their prices are also likely to fluctuate with the overall market for corporate shares, or the market for their industry. Market timing is the effort to buy when the market is at a low point of a cycle and sell when it is at its high point. *Money managers* who practice market timing have generally had a worse record than those who use a random selection method.

Media The means by which a message is delivered. Popular *direct public offering* media include *direct mail*, radio, newspapers, magazines, and seminars.

Merge and purge A *database management* tool. Computer programs will combine two or more lists of *prospects*, reorder them and eliminate duplications. The process is called merge and purge.

Merit state A state with *blue sky laws* requiring that an offering of *securities* must meet a quality standard, such as *fair, just and equitable.*

Minimum/maximum offering In a *best efforts underwriting* or a *direct public offering*, there may be a minimum and a maximum number of *shares* offered for sale. If orders are received for less than the minimum during the offering period, then the offering is cancelled and any money received is returned (funds are usually required to be deposited in escrow). If offers are received for more than the maximum, then shares may be prorated among investors.

Money manager or investment advisor For *individual investors*, a *financial planner* may be considered their money manager. If they have given discretionary authority to their financial planner or *broker*, then decisions about when and how much to buy, sell, and even borrow, can be made by them without any consultation. Most institutions give this discretionary authority to their investment advisors who are usually referred to as money managers.

Narrowcasting In contrast to broadcasting, this is use of *media* that primarily reaches only certain *target markets*. It most often refers to the use of cable TV. Through *market segmentation*, a *proposition* can be communicated through a cable channel that *market research* shows is watched by a significant number of the likely *prospects* for a *direct public offering*.

NASD (National Association of Securities Dealers) All *securities firms* included in *underwriting syndicates* belong to the NASD, which is a *self-regulatory organization*. The *SEC* recognizes regulation by the NASD as a substitute for what the government would otherwise have to police. Tests for *registered representatives, broker-dealer* principals, and other *securities* professionals are administered by the NASD.

NASDAQ (National Association of Securities Dealers' Automated Quotation System) This is an electronic display system but not a *stock exchange.* It allows subscribers to see the *bid* and *asked* prices quoted by each *market maker* for a company's *shares*, as well as certain trading history. Any orders are then placed by a separate communication.

National Quotation Bureau, Inc A subsidiary of Commerce Clearing House Inc. Publisher since 1913 of the *Pink Sheets*, the daily printed lists of 10,000 to 12,000 *over-the-counter market* shares and the most recent *bid* and *asked* quotations announced by their *market makers*. Before *NASDAQ* and the *OTC Bulletin Board*, this was the only source of information about *shares* which are not listed for trading on a *stock exchange*.

Net worth The *shareowners' equity* in a corporation. Through double entry bookkeeping, it equals assets less liabilities. It results primarily from money invested by *shareowners* and the earnings (or losses) not paid out in *dividends*.

New issue Any security being sold by the company issuing it. A *primary market* transaction rather than a sale by an investor-owner into the *secondary market*.

Niche marketing Directing a marketing program at a particular group of *prospects* who fit defined characteristics and are seen as neglected by competitors. A niche is selected and described through *market segmentation*. It is a step beyond selecting *target markets*, because the search is for prospects that are in an overlooked niche.

No-action letter This is a letter from the staff of the *SEC* saying that it will not recommend enforcement action. A no-action letter is issued in response to a request by lawyers for the company, prepared because they are uncertain whether some proposed steps are in violation of the securities laws. The no-action letter is limited to the facts presented in the letter request. However, the SEC releases most no-action letters for publication and lawyers often use them to support their own opinion to clients. As a matter of published policy, the SEC will not issue no-action letters on certain types of questions.

North American Securities Administrators Association (NASAA) State agencies administering *blue sky laws* belong to NASAA, where efforts are made to coordinate enforcement against fraud and to achieve some uniformity in the rules governing the sale of *securities*.

Offering circular The information or disclosure document by which an offer of *securities* is made to *prospects*. It is the same type of document as a *prospectus*—the different name results from the term used in the applicable securities laws. For instance, a security registered under the federal *Securities Act of 1933* would be offered by a prospectus, while one filed under the *Regulation A* exemption from that Act would use an offering circular.

Offering expenses Costs incurred by the company for the purpose of the *public offering*. Major offering expenses include legal and accounting fees. Internal costs, such as an allocation of compensation and overhead for employees' time, are generally not shown in the filings under the securities laws. For an *underwritten public offering*, more than half the total offering expenses will be the *underwriting spread*, which may be subject to a maximum under *NASD* rules. The *SEC* requires disclosure of the *underwriting spread* and total offering expenses in the *prospectus*, with an itemization in the nonprospectus portion of the *registration statement*. Some *blue sky laws* in *merit states* set maximums on offering expenses, such as 15 percent of the total proceeds of the offering.

Offering price The price at which a security is offered for sale in a *public offering*. Because it is offered to the public, it is not practical to negotiate the price with *prospects*. In an *underwritten public offering*, the offering price is fixed by the *underwriting agreement* between the company and the *managing underwriter*, typically after orders have been taken for all the *shares* (at an estimated price or range). In a *direct public offering*, the price will have been set by the company's *board of directors* before the offering begins.

Officers and directors' questionnaire As part of the *under-writers'* and lawyers' *due diligence*, a lengthy list of questions is required to be answered in writing by the company's officers and directors.

Options Contracts allowing the owners to buy or sell *securities* at an agreed price and within an agreed time. In an *underwritten public offering*, the company will often grant options (also called *underwriters' warrants*), giving the *underwriters* the right to buy a *new issue* of the company's *shares* at any time within five years after the offering. The price is set at the minimum permitted by the *NASD* and *blue sky laws*—usually from 100 percent to 140 percent of the *offering price*.

OTC Bulletin Board An electronic information system started in June 1990. Initially available only to *NASD dealer* members who are *market makers* in *over-the-counter shares*, it displays names and telephone numbers of *market makers* in a company's *shares*. The *dealers* may or may not list firm or "unfirm" *bid* and *asked price* quotations. Rules for use of the OTC Bulletin Board are expected to evolve to make it similar to *NASDAQ*, with more firm quotations and much broader access.

Overallotment In an *underwriting syndicate*, the *managing underwriter* allots *shares* to be sold among the participating *securities firms*. The total number will initially be considerably more than shown in the *prospectus*, as the underwriters create a short position (selling more shares than they have agreed to purchase from the company). The reason for selling short is to cover *indications of interest* which become *reneges* after the *confirmations* are sent out to investors, as well as shares repurchased by the *underwriters* from *flippers* under a *stabilization bid*. If the amount of overallotment were to exceed the amount of reneges and *stabilization bid* repurchases, the *underwriting syndicate* would be forced to buy shares in the aftermarket in order to deliver shares sold in the *underwriting*. This could cause a *short loss*. That risk gave rise to the *Green*

Shoe option, which allows the *underwriters* to buy more shares at the *offering price* "to cover overallotments."

Over-the-counter shares Corporate *shares* which are not listed for trading on a *stock exchange*. There are an estimated 47,000 different issues of shares traded over the counter in the United States, according to the *NASD*. Of these, approximately 4,300 meet standards for quotation on *NASDAQ*. *Bid* and *asked* prices quoted by *market makers* for 10,000 to 12,000 issues are printed daily in the *Pink Sheets*. An increasing number of these are also available through computer terminals to subscribers of the *OTC Bulletin Board*.

Par value When *shares* are issued, they may be assigned a par value. This number no longer has any practical meaning, except that it must be less than the *offering price*. Many corporations now issue "no par" shares, assigning them instead a "stated value" for accounting purposes.

Partial public offering Selling *shares* in part of a business by having a subsidiary corporation *go public*. This is currently being done with subsidiaries operating in foreign countries, so that the shares can be marketed to residents there and traded on local *stock exchanges*. It could be especially appropriate for a *direct public offering*, where part of a business can be matched to *target markets* in another country.

Penny stocks Low-price *shares*, trading at anywhere from a fraction of $.01 to $5. A price movement that is very small in amount can represent a large percentage change. Penny stocks are the specialty of some *securities firms*, many of which have defrauded investors by manipulating the market and misrepresenting the facts.

Pink Sheets A 300-plus page book or electronic listing of about 10,000 to 12,000 corporate *shares* traded in the *over-the-counter market*. The name comes from the nonglare color of their original form. It's published once each business day. There are about 2,000 subscribers to the

Pink Sheets, which has been published by the *National Quotation Bureau Inc.* since 1913. The information is purchased by the *NASD* to display prices for some *shares* through its *OTC Bulletin Board.*

Poison pill A *shark repellent* device to discourage a hostile takeover of a controlling number of the company's *shares.* A poison pill is a right to buy *securities* of the corporation at a bargain price, with the right being triggered by a hostile takeover. It is intended to make the takeover too costly to be profitable.

Positioning A marketing strategy. It considers the frame of reference in the *prospects*' mind, then conveys an image to fit a particular mental position. The classic positioning is in contrast to a dominant competitor's product: "the Uncola," "We're No. 2," "IBM compatible." In a *direct public offering* it may be necessary to position corporate *shares* in reference to other investments (savings, real estate) or other ways to spend discretionary funds (automobiles, gambling). Then the particular company's distinguishing facts can be positioned within the *prospects*' understanding of the market, product, management, and competition. Positioning often comes after initial *market research* and *market segmentation*, but before planning the marketing program.

Posteffective period or quiet period The period after the *effective date* and before the *public offering* is considered to be over. During this time, any material changes in the information contained in the *prospectus* need to be disclosed, usually by *stickering the prospectus.*

Preferred shares A separate class of corporate *shares* having some preferential feature over *common shares.* Preferences often include a right to receive a percentage rate of *dividends*, to be repaid first if the corporation liquidates, or to elect a majority of the *board of directors* if performance standards are not met. Preferred shares may be voting or nonvoting and may or may not participate in *dividends* on *common shares.*

Prefiling conference A meeting with staff members of the *SEC* or state *blue sky laws* administrators, held before the filing of a *registration statement* for the proposed *public offering*. There may be a question as to whether the offering would meet the standards required by the laws, or whether some variation from usual practice may be used. Resolving these issues in a prefiling conference can prevent later delay or the receipt of a *bedbug letter* in response to a filing.

Prefiling period The time between a decision to make a *public offering* and the initial filing under the securities laws. Care must be taken not to do something inadvertently that could be considered *gun-jumping* during the prefiling period.

Price/book ratio The market price of a company divided by its *book value*, either in total or on a per *share* basis. For a company in the business of investing in marketable *securities*, which are frequently "marked to market" on the company's accounting records, book value can be a measure of real or market value; for most companies, however, it is not that useful.

Price/cash flow ratio The market price of a company divided by the annual cash flow generated by the company. This is used by sophisticated analysts and investors, with varying interpretations and methodologies. "Cash flow" is the excess of cash received by a company during an accounting period over the amount paid out. It will differ from net earnings because nearly every company with *publicly traded shares* uses the accrual method of accounting, rather than the cash method. Some who use this ratio apply it to "free cash flow," meaning cash not required for debt retirement or asset replacement. Since there is no generally accepted definition or usage, comparisons can be misleading.

Price/earnings ratio The market price of a company divided by its annual earnings, either on an historical or projected basis. This information is readily available in published tables of *publicly traded shares* and has become the most common means of comparing one corporation's *share* price with another's, as well as comparing stages in the *stock market* for *market timing*.

Price/revenue ratio The market price of a company divided by its annual revenues, either on an historical or projected basis. Earnings may be thought of as unreliable for comparison, because they are so affected by the stage of a corporation's growth, by management policy and by accounting methods. Some investors prefer using total revenue for comparison.

Primary market The sale of a *new issue* of its *securities* by a corporation, in contrast to the sale of outstanding securities by their owner in the *secondary market*.

Private placement In the language of the federal securities laws, a sale of securities "not involving a public offering." Generally, a negotiated sale between a corporation and one or a few investors. An *investment banker* or other agent may be involved for a fee. There is a web of regulations and decisions about what is legally a *private placement*, since the securities laws dictating use of a *prospectus* do not apply.

Privatization When a government-owned business is transferred to nongovernment owners or operators. This can happen by contracting out a service formerly provided by government employees, or by negotiated sale of an operation. Privatizations through *initial public offerings* are occuring in nearly every part of the world, except North America. England and other countries have used consumer marketing campaigns to motivate the broadest individual purchase of *shares*.

Proceeds The amount received by the issuer from a *public offering* of *securities* (after the *underwriting spread* in an *underwritten public offering*). Net proceeds is the amount after payment of all other *offering expenses*. Securities laws require that the *prospectus* have a "Use of Proceeds" section, explaining what the issuer is going to do with the money received from investors.

Projections Estimates of the future operations and conditions for a business. They have been permitted and encouraged for many years, but almost never used in *prospectuses* for *underwritten public offerings* of *shares*. *Projections* are generally used in *private placements* of *shares* and in *public offerings* of *junk bonds*.

Promoter The founder or organizer of a corporate business. Securities law administrators often require the identity and background of promoters to be described in the *prospectus*.

Promotional shares *Shares* issued in return for services or ideas, usually when a business is first incorporated. Securities regulators look for full disclosure about promotional shares in the *prospectus*. Shares issued to founders or *promoters* at a nominal price within three years before filing the registration statement, will often be considered *cheap stock*, and it may be necessary for those shares to be kept in escrow for a period after the *public offering*.

Proposition In *direct marketing* parlance, this is the first stage—the offer to *prospects* of something they can request through a *response*.

Prospects Potential investors in the company's *shares*. In an *underwritten public offering*, they will be customers of *registered representatives* and those on lists used for *cold calling*. In a *direct public offering*, prospects may be people known to the company's employees and *directors*, names obtained through *market research* and *list brokers*. They may also be self-selected through their response to a *proposition* made in the *media*.

Prospectus The disclosure document by which a *public offering* of *securities* is made (sometimes known as an *offering circular*). The prospectus will be the major part of any filing with the *SEC* and with any state securities regulators under the *blue sky laws*. Its contents are prescribed by rules, forms, and instructions. In *underwritten public offerings*, a *prospect* does not see the prospectus until after placing an order to buy *shares*. It has often been said that only three kinds of people ever read the prospectus: the lawyers and accountants who prepare it, the SEC and blue sky laws staff assigned to review it, and the securities litigation attorneys hired to recover money lost from buying the shares. As a result of this view of the prospectus as a "liability document," it is generally very long and very difficult to read. In a *direct public offering*, the prospectus is the *fulfillment* of the prospect's *response* to the company's *proposition*. It is the principal selling tool, intended to be read before a decision is made to buy shares. To be effective it must be readable and interesting. This requires some change in the habits of securities lawyers and regulators.

Public offering When *securities* are offered for sale to the public rather than in a negotiated *private placement*. The basic rule of the *Securities Act of 1933* is that no public offering may be made (unless an exemption applies) until delivery of a *prospectus*—and then only after the *effective date* of the *registration statement*, which includes the prospectus. There is a gray area into which companies may inadvertently stumble, where private becomes public in violation of the securities laws. This may be uncovered during the *corporate cleanup, due diligence*, or *regulatory review*, and can require a *rescission offer*.

Public relations Communications to the public in *media* that are not directly paid for, as opposed to advertising. It includes being mentioned in articles written by journalists, being featured on radio, TV news or feature programs, and other more subtle ways of having "independent" third parties convey facts or images which originated with the company. It can be done in ways that are entirely legal and ethical. While the cost may be much lower than purchasing media usage, the company probably has little control over the content of the message and the market to which it is distributed. The use of public relations in a *public offering* is made particularly sensitive by the risk of *gun-jumping*, that is, influencing *prospects* before they have received a copy of the *prospectus*.

Publicly traded shares *Shares* that are available in the *secondary market* through a *securities firm.* Trading may occur through listing on a *stock exchange* or price quotation in the *over-the-counter market.* When few trades occur, shares are considered to be "thinly traded." Where it is necessary for a *broker* to make calls in order to find a match for a prospective buyer or seller, there is a "work out market," or a "market by appointment." There are numerical standards for *publicly traded shares* set by the *stock exchanges, NASDAQ,* and the *Securities Exchange Act of 1934.* They include having a minimum number of *shareowners* and a required *float.*

Qualify This has two different meanings in *public offerings.* To qualify shares under a state's *blue sky laws* means to meet the requirements for a *public offering* to that state's residents. To qualify the *prospects* for a share offering means to determine that they then have the interest and the *suitability* to invest in the *shares.*

Quiet period A period of up to 90 days after the *effective date* of an *IPO,* during which a *prospectus* may have to be delivered to buyers in the *secondary market.* Special care is necessary for any other written communications, especially if they are not preceded or accompanied by a prospectus.

Recirculation Providing another *prospectus* to persons who received an earlier version. This may be required for people who were provided a *red herring.* It may become necessary as a result of *stickering the prospectus* or having to print an amended prospectus.

Red herring A preliminary *prospectus* that has been filed with the *SEC,* but is used before its *effective date.* The name comes from the legend required to be printed on the cover, in red ink, to the effect that it is not a final prospectus. *Shares* can not be offered by the red herring and anyone receiving the red herring must later be given a final prospectus.

Regional exchange One of the six *stock exchanges* in the United States, other than the New York and the American.

They include the Boston, Cincinnati, Midwest, Pacific, Philadelphia, and Spokane.

Registered representative An individual licensed to act as agent for a *broker-dealer* in buying and selling *securities* for the account of others. Also known as *"brokers," "stockbrokers," "account executives," "financial planners," "financial consultants,"* and *"investment representatives."* At most *securities firms*, the registered representatives keep from 35 percent to 75 percent of the commissions generated on their transactions. Discount brokers pay their registered representatives a salary to process orders from customers without giving advice or participating in the investment decision.

Registered shares Corporate *shares* covered by a *registration statement* filed with the *SEC*. When shares are registered for a *public offering* under the *Securities Act of 1933*, it is only for the purposes of that offering. When a corporation's shares meet the standards for being considered as *publicly traded*, they must be registered under the *Securities Exchange Act of 1934*.

Registrar The keeper of the records showing the ownership of *shares*. It is now a combined function with the *transfer agent*, which records transfer of shares from one owner to another. A company may act as its own registrar and transfer agent or may contract the service to a bank corporate trust department, or a data services company.

Registration statement A filing required by the *SEC* for a *public offering* under the *Securities Act of 1933* or for *publicly traded shares* under the *Securities Exchange Act of 1934*.

Regulation A An exemption made by the *SEC* from filing a *registration statement* under the *Securities Act of 1933*. It applies to offerings below a certain dollar amount, which has changed over the years. It still requires much of the same filing material and process as a registration statement, but is processed through regional SEC offices, rather than Washington, D.C. (except for any number of interpretations for which the regional officials may have to send to Washington).

Regulatory review Review of the *registration statement* by the staff of the *SEC* and state *blue sky laws* administrators.

Reneges Cancellations by investors who have placed orders in an *underwritten public offering*. They will have expressed their *indication of interest* to a *registered representative* for a member of the *underwriting syndicate* or *selling group* before the *effective date*. They will then receive a *confirmation* with the *prospectus*. Within five days the investor must pay for the *shares*. Those who do not are reneges and the shares allotted to them come back to the underwriting syndicate.

Rescission offer An offer to existing *shareowners* to exchange their *shares* for return of the price they paid. A rescission offer is usually made only because the shares are considered to have been originally sold in violation of the securities laws. Most often this is discovered by the securities lawyers during the *corporate cleanup* or *due diligence*. A typical case is a series of share sales to small groups of investors without following the filing and *prospectus* delivery requirements for a *public offering*.

Response The object of a *direct marketing proposition* is to get a *response*, which occurs when the *prospects* request the *prospectus*.

Restricted shares Sale of restricted shares is limited, either because of who owns them (such as an *insider*), or because of the way they were acquired (such as in a *private placement*). The restriction may be imposed by the securities laws or by an agreement. When *shares* are used as incentive compensation to employees, they are often subject to a restriction that they can only be sold back to the company until a certain date or event.

Results/cost ratio Dividing the cost of a *direct marketing* program into the sales or other dollar measurement of results. This is often done with *test marketing*, the use of selected *media*, or lists of *prospects*.

Rights offering An offering of securities made only to persons who are already owners of the company's securities. The name comes from the day when it was common for a company's charter to give current holders the first right to acquire *new issues*. That provision is rare today, but many corporations find they can raise all the capital they need by asking their existing *shareowners* if they would like to buy more.

Risk factors A section near the front of a *prospectus*, calling attention to the most significant risks of loss from an investment in the company's *shares*. Usually required in *IPO*s.

Road Show Also known as *Dog and pony show*. In the last week or so before the *effective date* of an *underwritten public offering*, there is usually a road show. Top officers of the company, *investment bankers*, and perhaps lawyers and *auditors*, travel to meetings with *money managers* and representatives of the *underwriting syndicate*. These are usually conducted over the days' three meals, with smaller sessions for major *prospects*. Preparation for road shows is often very elaborate, with speech training, mock session rehearsals, video, and slide presentations. *Shares* can legally be offered only by the *prospectus*; however, that document is not yet available in required final form at the time of the road show. While the road show cannot lawfully provide any information that is not available to the entire public, it is typically the only marketing effort in which the company participates.

Safe Harbor Rules The *SEC* has issued interpretations for some of its rules, giving numerical and other objective standards. They are not the exclusive answers. However, if the facts of a particular situation fall within those standards, then the rules provide a "safe harbor" and the company does not need to get a *no-action letter* or other assurance that it will not violate the securities laws. There are, for instance, safe harbor rules with respect to the use of financial forecasts in a *prospectus*.

SCOR (the Small Corporate Offering Registration) Also known as *ULOR*, the Uniform Limited Offering Registration. It is a procedure for *public offerings* of *securities* in amounts of up to $1 million every 12 months. These "small offerings" are exempt from *SEC* registration only if they *qualify* under state *blue sky laws* that require delivery of a *prospectus* or *offering circular* to *prospects*. The form used by corporations has been approved by a committee of the American Bar Association and by *NASAA*. The SCOR rules had been adopted in 18 states through 1990.

SEC The United States Securities and Exchange Commission, which administers the federal securities laws.

Secondary market The *trading market* for securities that have been previously issued by a corporation. (The original issuance would have been an offering in the *primary market*).

Secondary offering An offering, generally through an *underwriting*, of securities already issued and owned by a *selling shareowner*. This occurs when the number of *shares* to be sold is considered too large for the *trading market* to absorb without harmful effects on the market price. A secondary offering is often included with a *primary offering* made at the same time by the company. When there is a secondary offering included in the *initial public offering*, some investors believe it shows a lack of faith and an effort by the selling shareowners to bail out. The term secondary offering is frequently misused to apply when a company makes its second *public offering*.

Securities There has been considerable litigation over what are securities, especially in the areas of real estate transactions, borrowings, and joint ventures. Corporate *shares* are clearly within the definitions of securities.

Securities Act of 1933 Amended from time to time, this law is the federal structure governing *public offerings* of *securities*, the *primary market*. It is administered by the *SEC*.

Securities Exchange Act of 1934 (There is no "and" in the title, as there is in the "Securities and Exchange Commission.") Amended from time to time, this law is the federal structure governing the trading of *securities*, the *secondary market*. It defines and governs *stock exchanges*, *securities firms*, and other participants in the securities markets.

Securities firm A business which acts as a *broker*, *dealer*, or *investment banker*.

Securities fraud Transactions in *securities* are subject to the same laws concerning fraud as other types of commerce. In addition, the securities laws make certain specific actions subject to criminal prosecution, to *SEC* "cease and desist" enforcement, and to actions for damages by persons claiming loss. These are referred to as securities fraud.

Selected dealer agreement Large *public offerings* often require a broader *telemarketing* network than all the *registered representatives* employed by members of the *underwriting syndicate*. Other *securities firms* will be invited to sell a specific number of *shares* in return for the *selling concession* portion of the *underwriting spread*. They sign a selected dealer agreement, which becomes effective when the *underwriting agreement* is signed.

Self-regulatory organization (SRO) A trade group recognized by the *SEC* as capable of enforcing rules about fairness of the *securities* markets. Principal *SROs* are the *stock exchanges* and the *NASD*.

Selling concession The portion of the *underwriting spread* paid to the *securities firm* employing the *registered representative* who actually sells *shares* in an *underwritten public offering*. The selling concession is typically 60 percent of the *underwriting spread*.

Selling group The *securities firms* who sell *shares* in an *underwritten public offering*, but not as members of the *underwriting syndicate.* They sign a *selected dealer agreement* and receive a *selling concession* for shares they sell.

Selling materials Any written, filmed, recorded, or broadcast materials used in selling the *shares* other than the *prospectus.* Except for a very limited announcement of the proposed *public offering,* no selling materials may be communicated to *prospects* until after the *effective date,* and then only if they are preceded or accompanied by a final prospectus. During this *free writing period,* the *fulfillment* package will include selling materials along with the prospectus. Additional selling materials will be used in the follow-up efforts for *conversion.*

Selling shareowners In a *secondary offering,* the persons selling their *shares* in the company.

Settlement date When payment for *securities* is due and certificates are to be delivered, generally five business days after the *confirmations* of sale are dated and mailed.

Shareowners Persons owning *shares* in a corporation. Also known as shareholders or stockholders.

Shareowners' equity The dollar amount of the *shareowners'* interest in the corporation, as shown on its accounting records. Also known as *net worth* or *book value.*

Shares Fractional ownership interests in a corporation. Shares are also called *stock.* There are *common shares* and *preferred shares.* They generally have the right to vote for the election of *directors* and on certain policy issues. Shares receive whatever *dividends* the *board of directors* decides should be paid. If the company is sold or liquidated, *shareowners* receive whatever is left over after payment to all creditors.

Shark repellants Legal devices used to prevent a *takeover* of a controlling number of a company's *shares.* They are intended to make the acquisition too costly for the outsider, thereby protecting the *insiders.*

Shelf offering A *public offering* of *securities* which have been through the *effective date* of a *registration statement* and then held "on the shelf" until the company decides to offer them. This allows management to indulge in *market timing*, trying to sell securities when the terms are most favorable to the company. It also encourages *bought deals*, where *underwriters* come to the company after they have already arranged for the buy side of a transaction.

Shell corporation A corporation with *publicly traded shares* but no operating business. This can happen when the business has been sold or discontinued without dissolving the corporate form. It also results from a *blind pool IPO*. By placing an operating business into the shell corporation, a business can *go public by the back door*.

Short loss Money lost by the *underwriting syndicate* as a result of selling more *shares* in the *underwriting* than it agreed to buy from the *issuer* (including shares purchased under the *Green Shoe option*). Twenty percent of the *underwriting spread* is intended to help defray any short loss (see *flipper*, *overallotment*, and *reneges*).

Short swing profits Once a company has *securities* registered under the *Securities Exchange Act of 1934*, officers, *directors*, and owners of more than 10 percent of the *shares* must file reports. They must also pay over to the company all "profits" resulting from any matching of sales and purchases of *shares* within any six-month period. This rule has nothing to do with intent and is often triggered accidentally.

Small cap stocks The *shares* of companies with a *market capitalization* of less than $50 million to over $100 million, depending on the line drawn by a *money manager*. Measurement may also be in terms of the *float*.

Soft dollar deals Arrangements where goods or services are provided to investors, usually *money managers*, in return for an understanding that the provider will be compensated in commissions from *securities* transactions. For instance, a *securities firm* may provide research services to a money manager. When that money manager buys *shares* in an *underwritten public offering*, it may instruct the *managing underwriter* to treat it as a *directed sale* so that the *selling concession* is paid to the provider of soft dollar services. Before Mayday 1975, when fixed commission rates were deregulated in the trading market, money managers used soft dollar deals to get volume discounts for their trades. Now, commissions in the *secondary market* have all been negotiated down by money managers to a fraction of their fixed level, leaving no room for discounts. The *underwriting spreads* on *bonds* have been similarly negotiated down by the large corporate borrowers, especially with the tools of *shelf offerings* and *bought deals*. (Rated bond public offerings that paid .875 percent are now sold at .25 percent or less. Unrated *junk bonds* were underwritten at 3.0 percent or more, but very few have recently been issued.) As a result, about the only vestige of pre-Mayday commission rates is in underwritten public offerings of shares, particularly *IPOs*, where the underwriting spread has actually increased from about 6 percent to 8 percent. Money managers are the major buyers of *underwritten initial public offerings* and use them extensively to make payments on soft dollar deals.

Specialist The *securities firm* assigned to make the market for a company's *shares* on a *stock exchange*. A specialist continuously announces *bid* and *asked prices* and generally owns an inventory of the shares. All trades in *listed shares*, by *brokers* or *dealers* who are members of the stock exchange, are required to go through the specialist (with increasing exceptions). The specialist is a dealer, buying and selling shares for the dealers' own account. This serves to maintain an inventory, allowing trades when there are no corresponding bid and asked prices being offered. It also allows the specialist to accumulate positions in the shares for an expected profit on future moves in the market.

Sponsor A person, group, or company standing behind an offering of *shares*. Investors can reasonably conclude that the sponsor has performed *due diligence* and has an economic stake in the company or its shares. In *underwritten public offerings*, the *managing underwriter* is usually thought of as a sponsor (and is referred to by that term in England). In a *direct public offering* there may be a large corporate *strategic partner* or *venture capitalist* who purchased shares of the company in an earlier *private placement* and whose name conveys *endorsement* or sponsorship. Arrangements can be made for a recognized name to be a sponsor through a *standby commitment*, by agreeing to buy all *shares* not purchased by *prospects* in the offering.

Stabilization bid A bid for *shares* made shortly after the *underwritten public offering* by a member of the *underwriting syndicate*. There is a specific exemption for this under the antimanipulation provisions of the securities laws. The purpose is to keep the market price from falling below the *offering price* until the underwriting syndicate has disposed of all the shares it committed to buy in the *underwriting agreement*.

Standby commitment An agreement to purchase any *shares* left over after completion of a *public offering*. This is commonly done in a *rights offering*, where a standby *underwriter* agrees to purchase all shares not subscribed for by the existing *shareowners*. Initially, the function of an *underwriter* in a public offering was to insure that all the money would be raised by issuing a standby commitment. It was akin to a performance bond. Today, there is only a *letter of intent* between the underwriter and the company proposing to *go public*. The risk that the public offering will not occur, or that the *offering price* will decline substantially, is borne entirely by the company. It is not until hours before the *effective date*, after all the selling efforts have been completed, that the contemporary underwriters will sign an *underwriting agreement* to buy the shares at an agreed price.

Statutory underwriter Someone who has become an *underwriter* within the meaning of the securities laws, even if that was not the intended status. The statutory definition of underwriter has sometimes been interpreted very broadly, especially where *securities fraud* has been alleged. Persons who purchased *shares* from the company or an *insider* and then resold them, may find they are a statutory underwriter. So may persons who provide services in a *public offering*. Since liability can arise solely out of the status of underwriter often without regard to intent, it is an important area for preventive law.

Stickering the prospectus Attaching a paper to the cover of a *prospectus* as a means of providing additional information. This is often required when material events occur after the *effective date*, but before the offering is concluded. It is an alternative to printing a new prospectus with amendments. Sometimes, the *SEC* will require recirculation of the revision to everyone who received the original prospectus. In rare circumstances, a *rescission offer* may be required.

Stock Another name for corporate *shares*.

Stock market The *trading market* for *shares* including the *stock exchanges* and the *over-the-counter market* (quoted on *NASDAQ*, the *OTC Bulletin Board*, or in the *Pink Sheets*). The *stock market* for *listed shares* is made by the assigned *specialist* for the stock exchange. For shares traded over-the-counter, one or more *securities firms* act as *market makers*. Beyond the stock exchanges and the over-the-counter markets, there are the so-called "third market" and "fourth market." The "third market" is made by *securities firms* who trade listed shares among themselves without going through a stock exchange. This *disintermediation* of the specialist is carried one step further in the "fourth market," where *money managers* trade among themselves without even going through a securities firm as *broker* or *dealer*.

Strategic partner A business which has bought *shares* in the company through a *private placement* for the dual purpose of making an investment return and helping its own business. Large corporations often become strategic partners of companies still in their development stage. This can provide access to new technology that complements the large corporation's products. It may give them access to a market they have not otherwise developed. In addition to investing capital, the strategic partner may also provide support services to the smaller business. Some entrepreneurs try to avoid having a strategic partner, feeling that they lose some independence in future policy decisions.

Street name When certificates for *shares* owned by an investor are issued and held in the name of a nominee. *Securities firms* often own all or part of a nominee corporation, used exclusively as the street name in which securities are held for its customers. The reason is to make *shares* more quickly available for transfer in the event they are sold. Sometimes, a *street name* is used to conceal the identity of the real owner from corporate management or others.

Suitability A test for whether someone really should be investing in a particular security. Checking suitability goes along with the *know-your-customer rule*. Several *blue sky laws* require that certain investments be offered only to persons meeting a set of *suitability* standards, usually related to wealth and income. Determining suitability is part of what it means to *qualify* a *prospect*.

Supermajority When a vote requires more than a majority of the *shares* owned by the *shareowners*. Provisions of the corporate charter may, in some states, provide that a merger or a recall of the *directors*, for instance, must be approved by 80 percent of the shares. The purpose is usually to create a *shark repellant* in order to prevent a *takeover*.

Takeover The transfer of a controlling interest in a corporation, usually by a purchase of more than half its outstanding *shares*. Although there can be a friendly takeover, the term usually refers to a hostile takeover. The best protection against a takeover is having a broad base of individual *shareownership* and a share price in the *trading market* that does not represent a bargain when compared to the company's "real value." *Shark repellants* are used as defenses against takeovers, but they are generally perceived as being for the benefit of management rather than *shareowners*.

Tangible book value The *book value* (also known as *shareowners' equity* and *net worth*) after adjustment by subtracting the recorded amount for such intangibles as goodwill. It is intended to represent the "hard assets" of the company less its liabilities.

Target markets *Prospects* for buying the company's *shares* organized into groups with similar characteristics, such as place of residence, occupation, or other *demographics*. The target markets are defined through *market segmentation*.

Telemarketing Using the telephone as a means of marketing. This has been virtually the only *media* employed in *underwritten public offerings*, where *securities firms* have their *registered representatives* telephone *prospects* to announce the offering, make a sales presentation, and take an order—preferably all in one call. In a *direct public offering*, telemarketing is one component of the marketing program. It may be passive (limited to answering incoming *responses* from *prospects* to the *proposition*) or active (initiating follow-up calls to prospects, after the *fulfillment* for their *conversion* into a sale). Careful procedures must be prepared and supervised to avoid violation of the securities laws, especially if the telemarketing staff are not *registered representatives* under the supervision of a registered *broker-dealer*.

Test marketing A limited offering of *shares* to a *target market*, using particular *media* or copy or graphic presentation. The purpose is to refine the marketing program as quickly and cost-effectively as possible.

Time and responsibility schedule A listing of all the steps to be accomplished in preparing and completing a *public offering*, together with the time by which the step is to be accomplished and the name of the person responsible for seeing that it is done.

Tombstone ad A formal announcement of a proposed or completed *public offering*. In an *underwritten public offering*, the tombstone ad typically appears only after the sale is completed. It advertises the names of the *underwriting syndicate* and shows that the *managing underwriter* has originated and completed a deal. The name tombstone ad comes from the sparse copy and the layered format. In a *direct public offering*, a tombstone ad can be used to announce a forthcoming offering. After the *effective date*, a tombstone ad can be used as the *proposition* stage of a direct public offering, promising to deliver a copy of the *prospectus* to the reader. It will contain a coupon, address and a telephone and facsimile number for the response. In a *broker-assisted* offering, the tombstone ad may suggest calling any of the participating *securities firms* or *financial planners*.

Trading market Where *publicly traded shares* are bought and sold. The *secondary market*, which is made either by a *specialist* for *shares* listed on a *stock exchange* or by *market makers* for *over-the-counter shares*.

Transfer agent The keeper of records showing transfers of the record ownership of *shares*. This is generally combined with the *registrar* and may be performed by the company or an independent contractor.

ULOR (the Uniform Limited Offering Registration) Also known as *SCOR*. Available under some state *blue sky laws* for *public offerings* of not more than $1 million, which are then exempt from *SEC* registration.

Underwriter A *securities firm* that sells *securities* in an *underwritten public offering* and then purchases those securities from the issuer. The name came from the former practice, where the underwriter became legally obligated to buy the securities at a fixed price, well in advance of selling them to the public. In insurance terms, it underwrote the risk that the securities would not be sold to the public at a price higher than the underwriter agreed to pay the company.

Underwriters' warrants Also known as *options*. They are rights to buy *shares* of the issuer in the future at prices based upon the *offering price* in an *underwritten public offering*. They represent additional compensation to the *underwriters* beyond the *underwriting spread*. Their terms are usually for five years, with the option price starting at 100 percent of the *offering price* and increasing by 10 percent each year. These terms are limited by *blue sky laws* and the *NASD*, which also permit the warrants to cover no more than 10 percent of the number of *shares* in the *underwriting*.

Underwriting The process of doing an *underwritten public offering*.

Underwriting agreement The legal document which commits the *underwriters* to buy *securities* in an *underwritten public offering*. Typically signed just hours before the *effective date*—after orders for more than the entire offering have been obtained—it fixes the *offering price* and the *underwriting spread*, usually within a range stated in the *letter of intent*.

Underwriting spread The commission paid to the *underwriters* in an *underwritten public offering*. It is called "the spread" because it equals the difference between the *offering price* and the *proceeds* of the offering paid to the issuer before *offering expenses*. An underwriting spread is generally divided in these proportions: A 60 percent *selling concession* to the *securities firm* employing the *registered representative* who sold the *shares*; a 20 percent "management fee" to the *managing underwriter*; and 20 percent for the "syndicate account," which pays the *underwriters'* expenses and applies toward any *short loss*.

Underwriting syndicate The group of *securities firms* which have signed an *agreement among underwriters* to sell a specified amount of an *underwritten public offering* and to bear a proportion of the *underwriters'* risks and expenses. Most of the selling is done through *telemarketing* by employees of syndicate members.

Underwritten initial public offering A company's first *public offering* of its shares, which it has chosen to do through an *underwriting.*

Underwritten public offering An offering of *securities* to the public, using a *securities firm* as an *underwriter.* The securities are sold by *registered representatives* of the underwriters to *prospects* they have selected. Selling occurs through *telemarketing.* If sufficient orders are collected for the securities, an *underwriting agreement* is signed. A week later there is a *closing,* where the underwriters pay the company the *offering price* for the *shares* less their *underwriting spread* and expenses.

Venture capital Money invested in a business in its early stages, when the risk of loss is generally greater and there is usually no *trading market* into which *securities* can be sold. There are stages of *venture capital* investment, from start-up or seed capital to second-round or sprout capital, mezzanine financing, and on to succeeding rounds. A venture capitalist—the investor—needs a potential exit from the investment, usually either a *public offering* or a sale of the entire business. Venture capitalists may be friends and relatives of the entrepreneur, venture capital firms, individual *angel investors (informal investors),* or other corporations as *strategic partners.*

Videotex Use of a video monitor for the *direct marketing* of products and services. Information may be transmitted by cable TV installations to the *prospects'* television receivers, through telephone installations to the prospects' computers, or by the prospects' operation of the keyboard at a retail site. Most *videotex* only delivers the *proposition*; a prospect's *response* comes through telephone, personal appearance, or other *media. Interactive marketing* through videotex will be particularly useful for *direct public offerings,* with the *prospectus* instantly accessible to prospects. The proposition, response, *fulfillment,* and *conversion* could take place during a single on-line interaction. New "multimedia" cards for personal computers allow the user to combine digital transmission from a computer with images from television, videodisk, or VCR. This will allow a completely electronic fulfillment package of the textual prospectus and graphic *selling materials.*

Waiting period The time between the filing of a *registration statement* with the *SEC* (or application to *qualify* shares under *blue sky laws*) and the *effective date* of that filing. Because there is no final *prospectus* available, no sales of *shares* can be made. Care must be taken to avoid *gun-jumping*, although the rules are somewhat different from the *prefiling period*. For instance, oral statements are permitted, even if they would be considered offers to sell *shares*. Video and slide presentations of company officers talking may be allowed, especially if the officers are available in person for questioning.

When-as-and-if-issued market (WAII market) When a *public offering* of *securities* is expected, a *trading market* will sometimes develop in advance. In periods when there have been many *hot new issues*, speculators have bought and sold *shares* with payment and delivery to be made when, as, and if the shares are actually issued. This is a form of risk *arbitrage*, where the participants are predicting the *offering price* and the subsequent price in the *trading market*.

Wire house A large *securities firm* with multiple offices serving retail (*individual investor*) customers. The name is from the days when orders for trading *securities* were transmitted to New York headquarters by a proprietary telegraph or telephone wire.

Index